Dazzling

Gianni A. Sarcone &
Marie J. Waeber

Sterling Publishing Co., Inc.
New York

Library of Congress Cataloging-in-Publication Data Available

1 3 5 7 9 10 8 6 4 2

Published by Sterling Publishing Company, Inc.
387 Park Avenue South, New York, N.Y. 10016
© 2002 by Gianni A. Sarcone and Marie J. Waeber
Distributed in Canada by Sterling Publishing
c/o Canadian Manda Group, One Atlantic Avenue, Suite 105
Toronto, Ontario, Canada M6K 3E7
Distributed in Great Britain and Europe by Chris Lloyd at Orca Book
Services, Stanley House, Fleets Lane, Poole BH15 3AJ, England.
Distributed in Australia by Capricorn Link (Australia) Pty. Ltd.
P.O. Box 704, Windsor, NSW 2756 Australia
Printed in China
All rights reserved

Sterling ISBN 0-8069-8393-0

Contents

Introduction

In English, there are two essential words to express the faculty and the act of seeing : 1) see, 2) view. The etymological sense of the words 'see' and 'view' are "to follow something with the eyes" (from the Indo-European **seq**) and "to have learned" (from the Indo-European **weid**). So, for our ancestors an image was something to shape with the eye (follow with the eye) and information taken from the real world (having learned from visual perception).

Unfortunately (or fortunately?), seeing isn't necessarily the direct perception of reality. Actually our brains are constantly interpreting and giving structure to the visual input from our eyes. If this were not the case, we wouldn't see any colors, and we would probably see the world upside down! Another interesting every-day paradox of our vision is that we don't see the edges of our visual field! In fact, we should see black zones outside of our visual field, but our brains cancel out these zones with a smooth fade-out effect.

In this book we have included classic and new optical illusions that will delight children and grown-ups as well as inquisitive minds in search of solid, accessible material on this amazing subject.

Vision isn't always WYSIWYG!

About the Authors

Gianni A. Sarcone and Marie J. Waeber, designers and writers, are talented specialists in creative learning. They develop educational manipulatives and thinking games that help teach mathematics and the visual and plastic arts. Their maxim is: "Be curious first!"

Chapter 1

Color and shade oddities

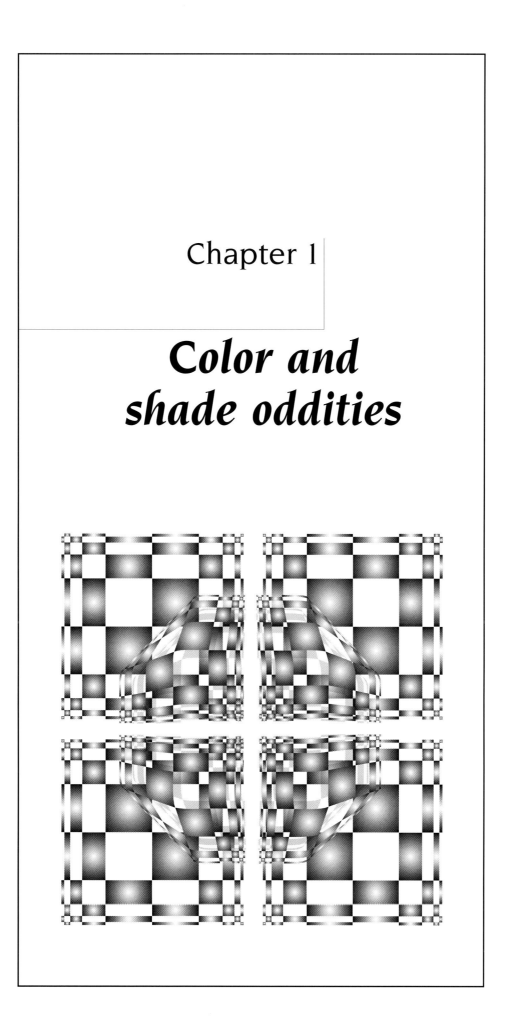

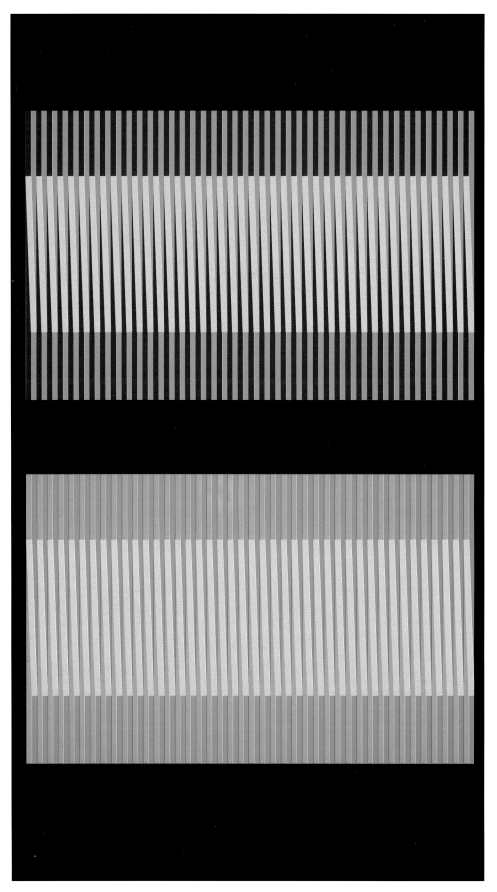

A color experiment with two colors and gray.
Do you see more than two colors?

With only two or three colors and white and black backgrounds,
we can create a huge variety of subjective tints and shades!

Sheen effect

(The squares seem to stand out against the background.)

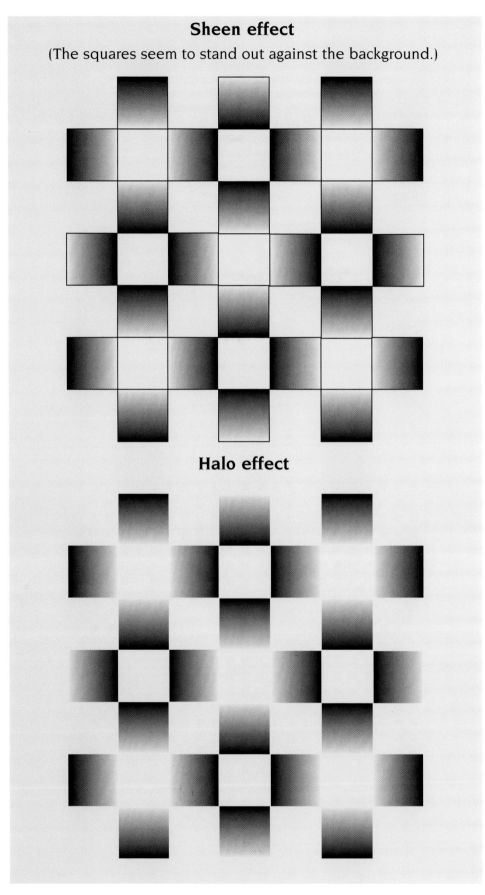

Halo effect

Using the same square composition with and without outlines,
we can obtain two very different effects.

Are all the gray squares the same shade?

How many different shades of red do you see in each diagram? If you answer five, you're wrong: the upper picture has four, the bottom, only three.

12

In each diagram, do you see one shade of red?
Or do you see darker and lighter shades?

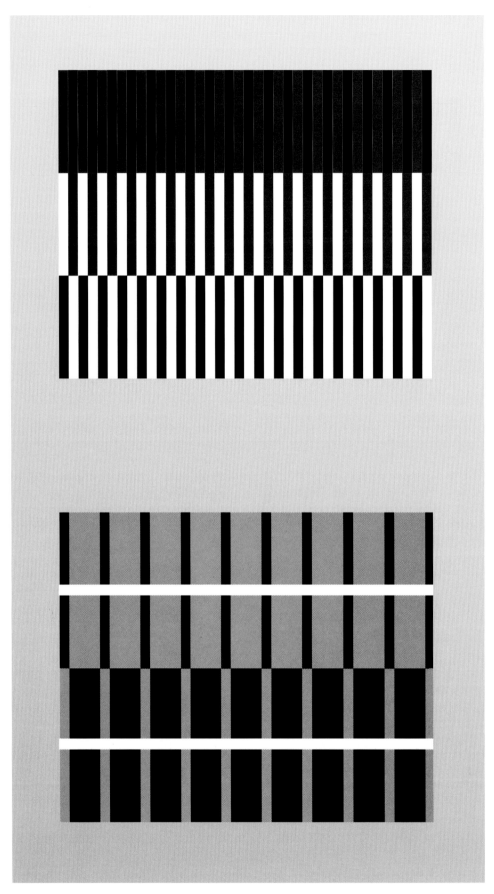

Shade illusions: Look at the white lines in the diagrams.
Do you see shades of pink and soft green?

Shade illusions II:
Are the wavy lines red and green?

Close one eye and stare at the yellowish dot
for 20 seconds to make it gradually disappear.

Here, you have to focus your attention on the
blue point to make the Cheshire cat vanish!

A marked white ring is sufficient to disrupt the fading
effect. Now it's difficult to complete the experiment.

Color fading

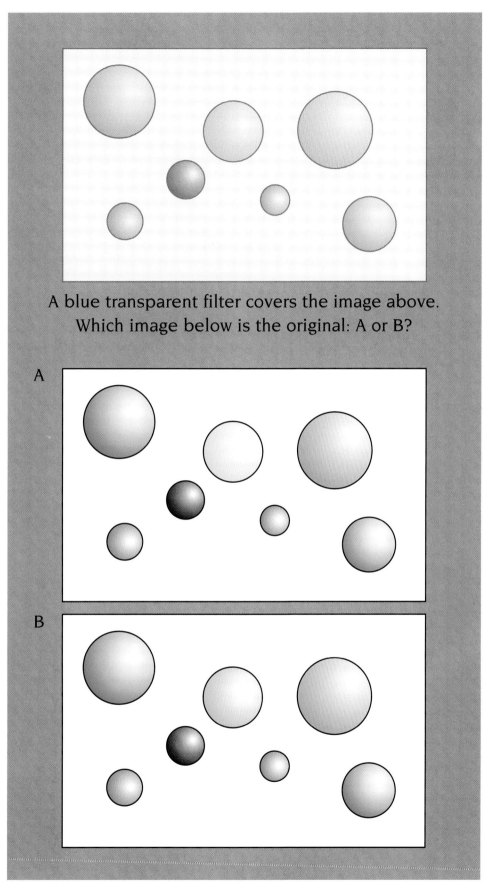

A blue transparent filter covers the image above.
Which image below is the original: A or B?

A

B

Color adaptation

The color in this photo of a cow is not well balanced; the left side is bluish and the right has too much yellow. To restore the color balance stare at the fly in the diagram below for 30 seconds, then look at the cow again. Does something change?

Color adaptation II

From a distance of 10 or 12 feet (3-4 meters), the small black dots along the edges of the squares seem to be blue and the white ones appear yellow.

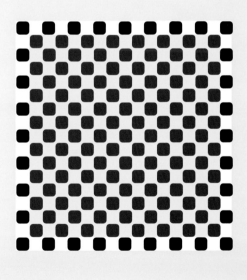

Color assimilation

Look at the duck from a distance of 6 feet (2 meters). Most people only see yellow inside the outline of the duck.

Color filling-in effect

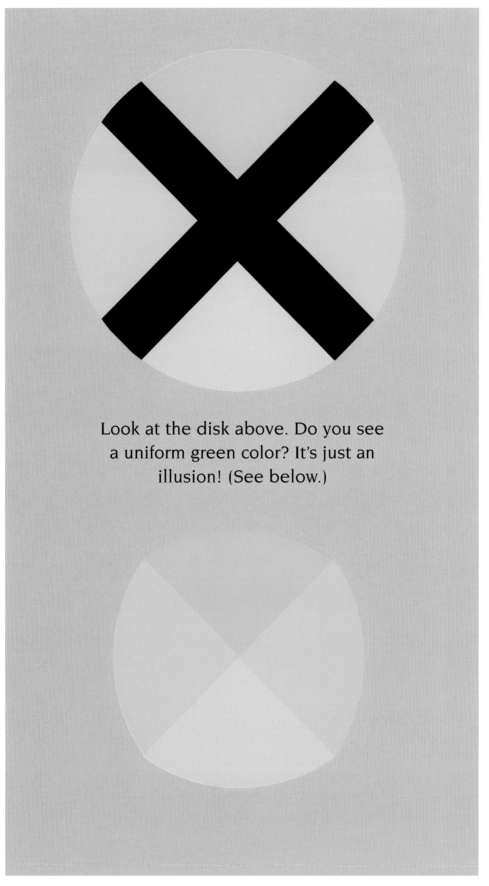

Look at the disk above. Do you see a uniform green color? It's just an illusion! (See below.)

Brightness illusion

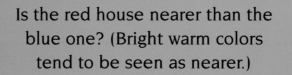

Is the red house nearer than the
blue one? (Bright warm colors
tend to be seen as nearer.)

Color influences

Look at both images. Has the kick-boxer
with the dark blue pants moved?

Shadow influences

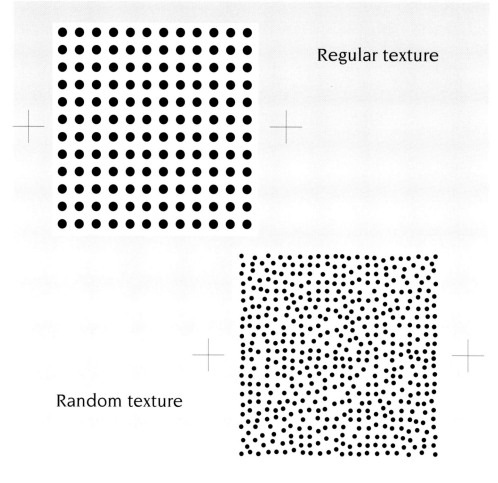

Regular texture

Random texture

Make a transparent photocopy of each texture above
and combine it with its original background to create
interesting moiré patterns.

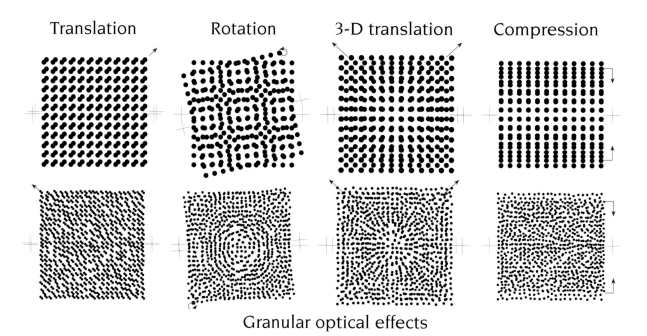

| Translation | Rotation | 3-D translation | Compression |

Granular optical effects

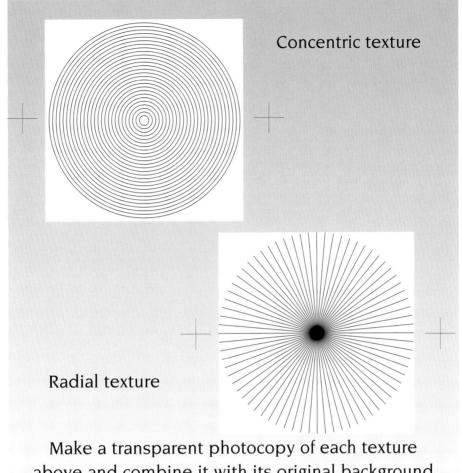

Concentric texture

Radial texture

Make a transparent photocopy of each texture
above and combine it with its original background
to create interesting moiré patterns.

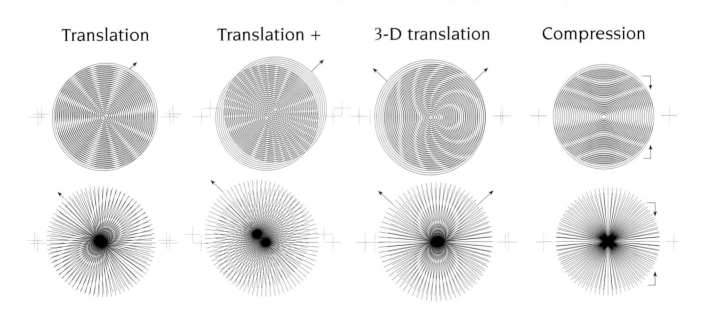

Translation   Translation +   3-D translation   Compression

Radiating optical effects

Below are depicted the 64 Yi King symbols, also called hexagrams. These antique signs are part of Chinese philosophy.

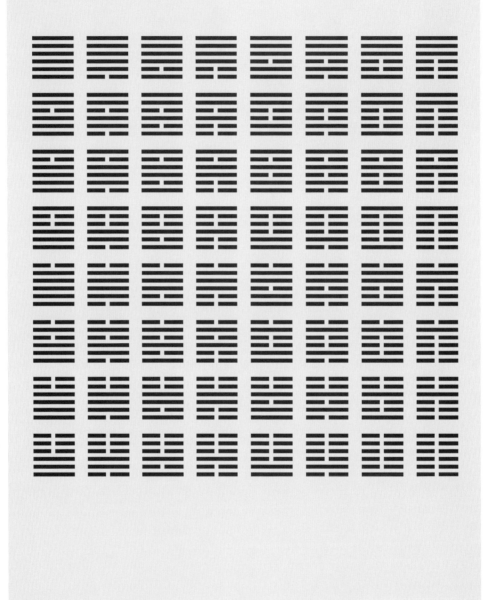

Do you see gray spots between the Yi King symbols?

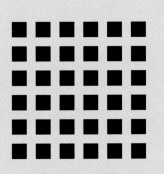

When the distance between the squares is small, you may see dark spots at the intersections.

When the distance is greater, you may see clear halos enveloping the squares.

In the image below the twinkling effect is increased. Black dots appear alternately when you move your eyes around the image.

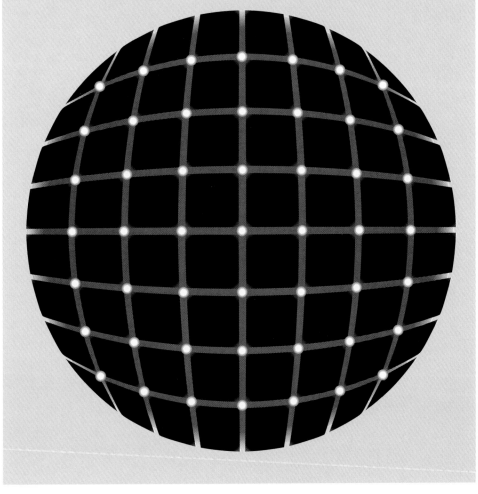

Phenomenal spots

Stare at the black point in the image above for 20 seconds, then quickly look at the white point below. A yellow zebra crossing will appear!

Color afterimage effect

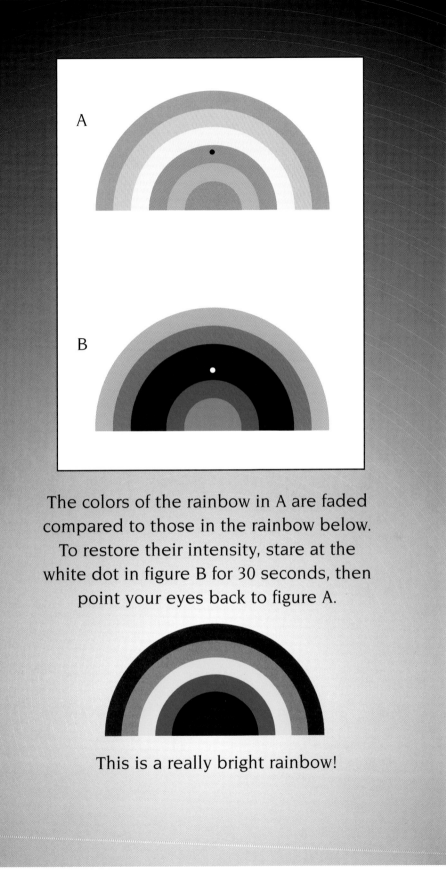

The colors of the rainbow in A are faded compared to those in the rainbow below. To restore their intensity, stare at the white dot in figure B for 30 seconds, then point your eyes back to figure A.

This is a really bright rainbow!

Selective afterimage effect

The yellow tile is
exactly the same in
all 3 diagrams!

The same color, in this case yellow, seems to change
when the hues of the bordering colors are altered.

The colors are exactly
the same in the
3 diagrams, only the
borderlines change!

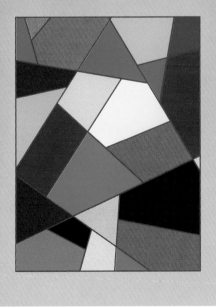

Borderlines can also subjectively modify
the hue of a color patchwork.

The black background seems slightly green in the triangle areas,
but that's just an illusion!

Solutions to Chapter 1

In this diagram there are 4 different hues.

Here, there are only 3 different hues.

All the gray squares are the same shade.

The background of the picture is a uniform red!

The small red squares are all the same hue.

The original image is on the left
The image on the right has the blue transparent filter.

Chapter 2

Geometric illusions

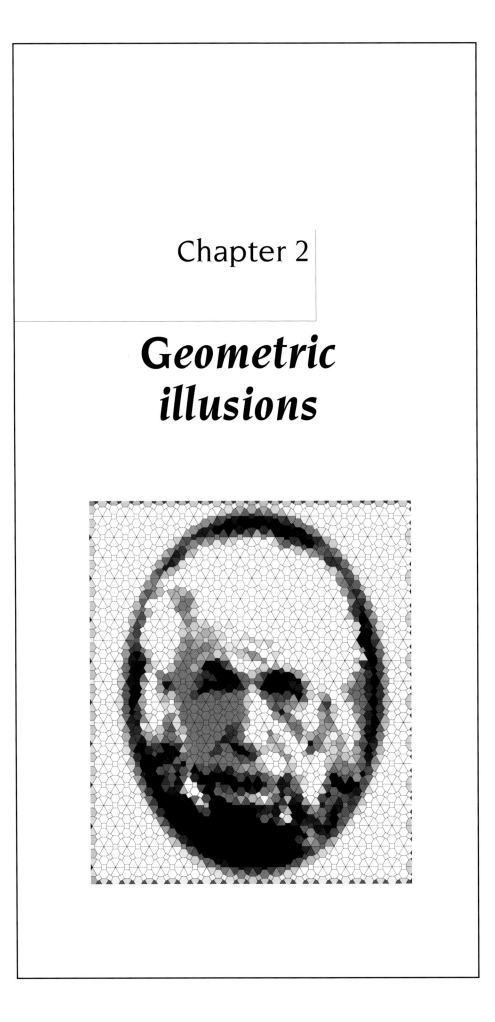

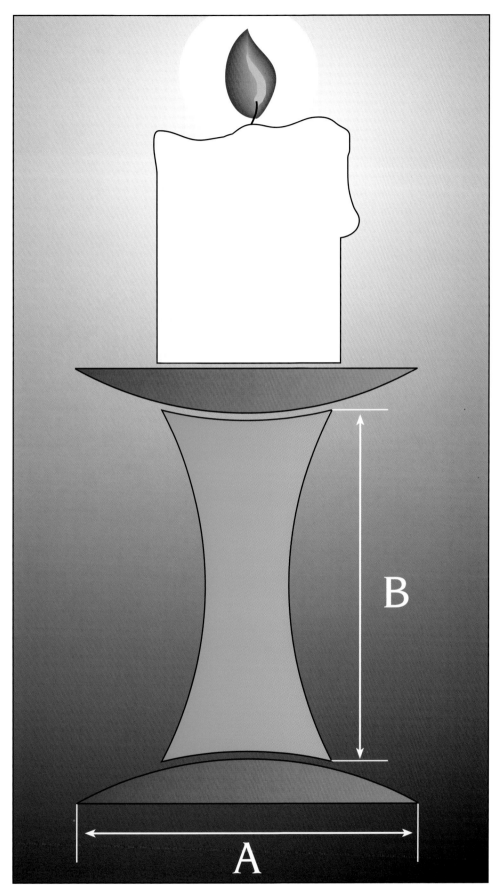

Which is correct: a) A = B   b) A > B   c) A < B

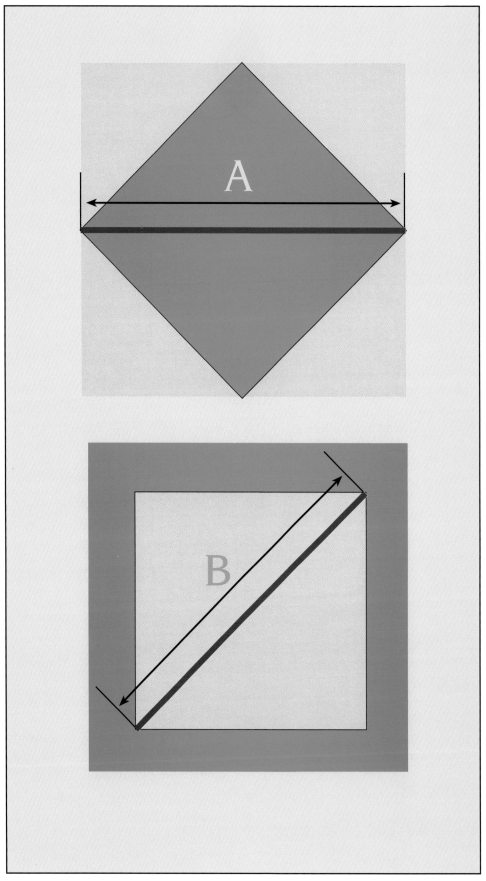

Which is correct: a) A = B   b) A > B   c) A < B

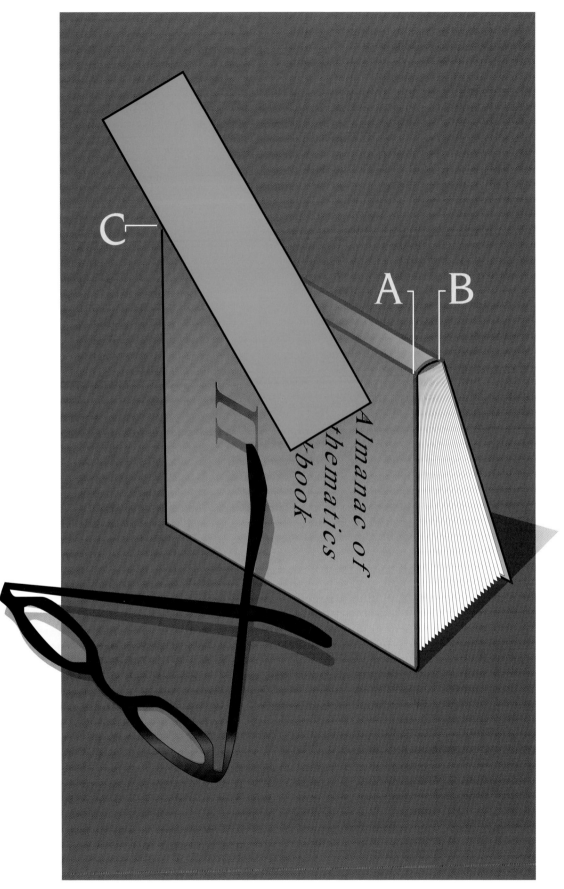

Which red line, A or B, is connected to point C?

Which line seems longer, the red one or the blue?

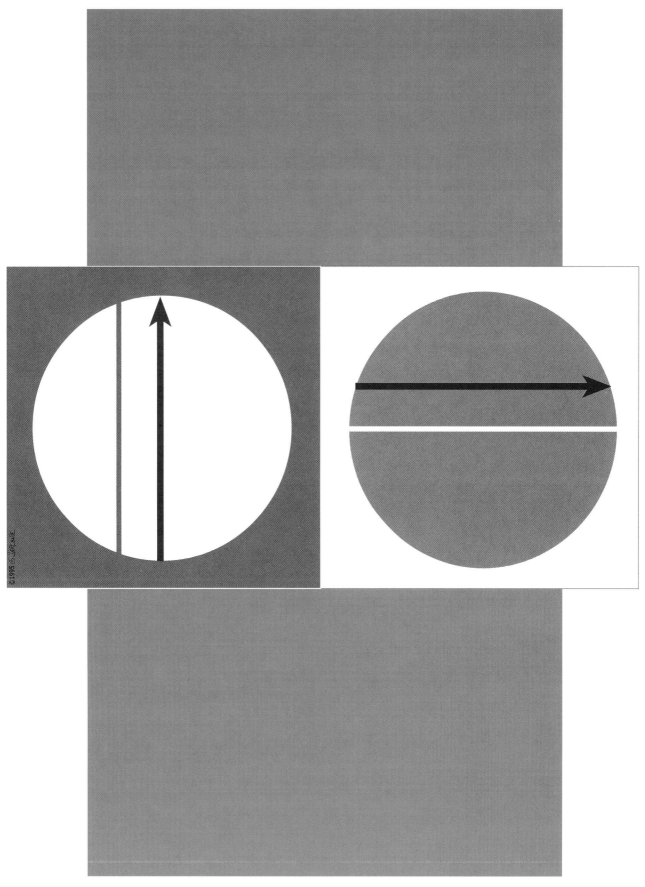

Is the red arrow longer or shorter than the blue one?

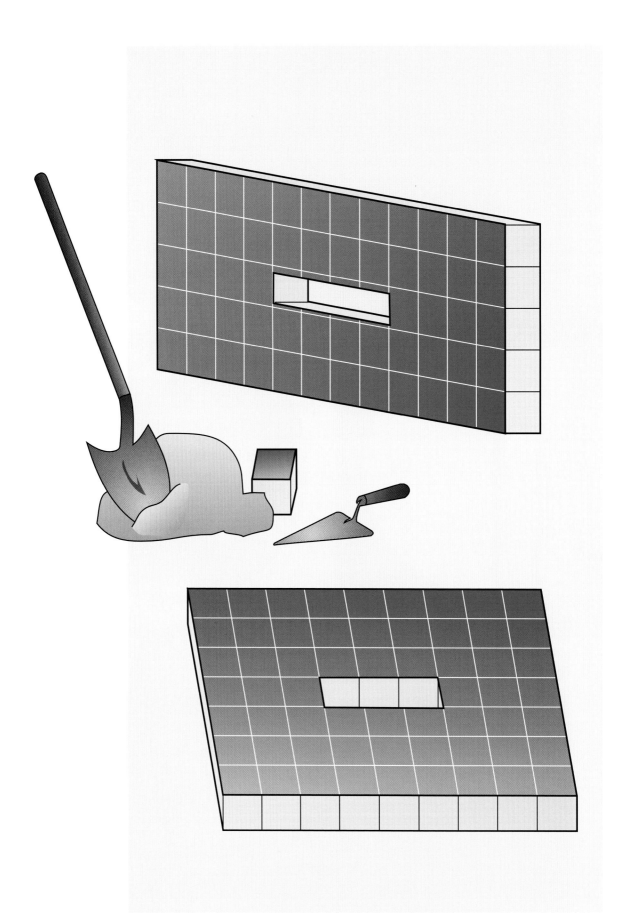

Are the blue surfaces different?

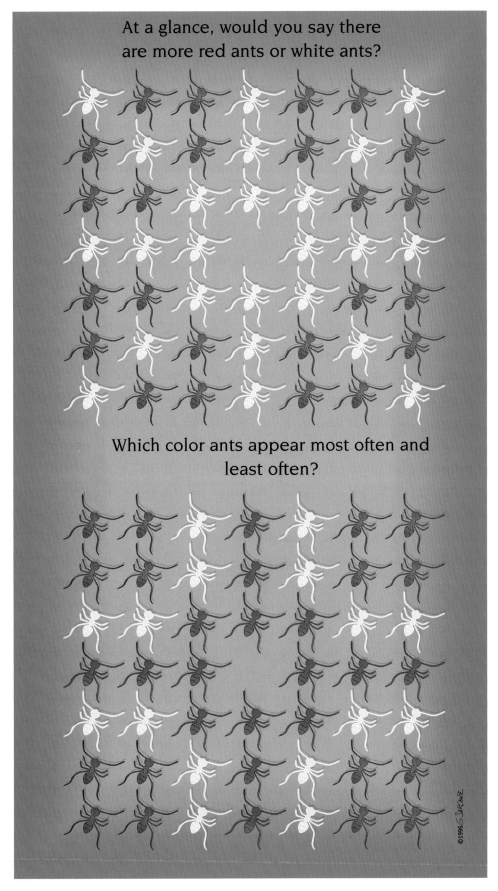

At a glance, would you say there are more red ants or white ants?

Which color ants appear most often and least often?

Ants reckoning

How many squares are there in this diagram?

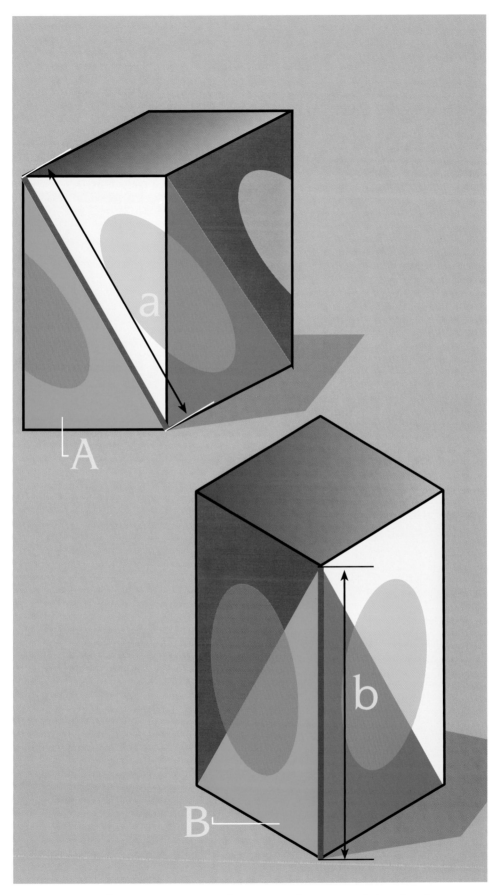

Are the green triangles A and B equal in size?
Are the red lines a and b the same length?

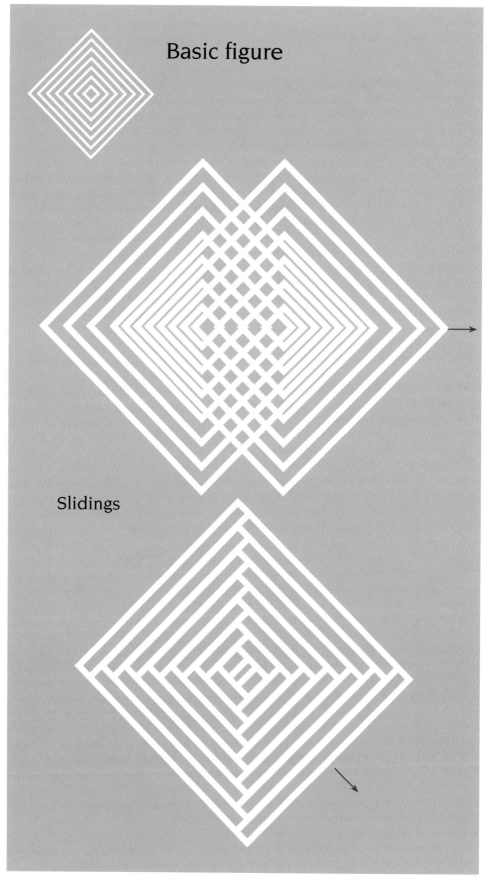

Basic figure

Slidings

Geometric optical effects with concentric squares

44

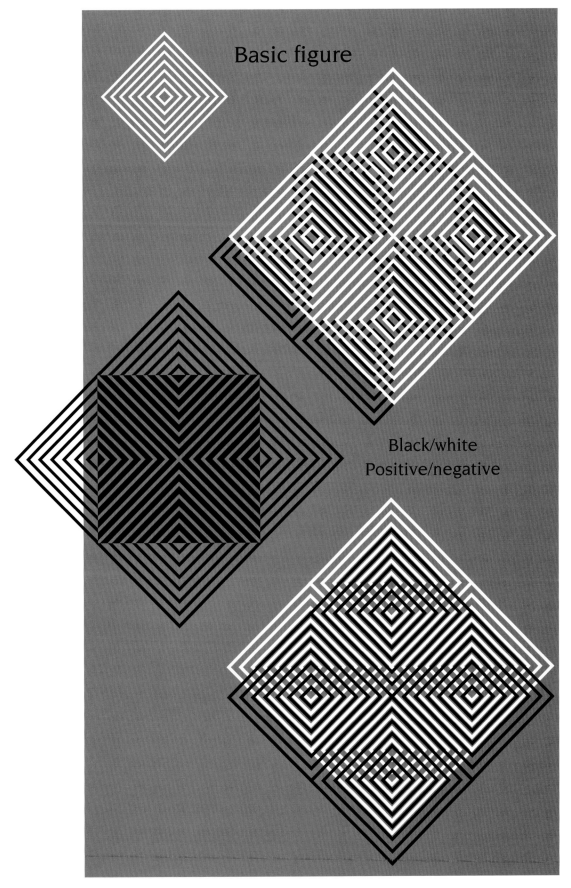

Basic figure

Black/white
Positive/negative

Geometric optical effects with concentric squares II

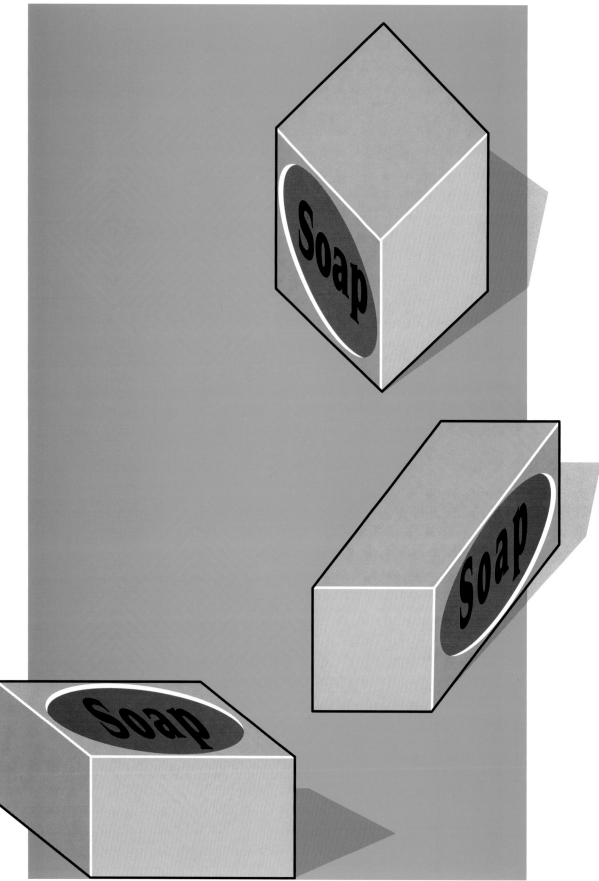

Are the red labels of the three soaps different sizes?

A simple pattern that creates great optical effects

Find in the diagram below:
a) 3 geometric shapes with the same areas
b) 3 geometric shapes with the same perimeters
c) 2 geometric shapes with the same surfaces

What do the 3 colored shapes below
have in common?

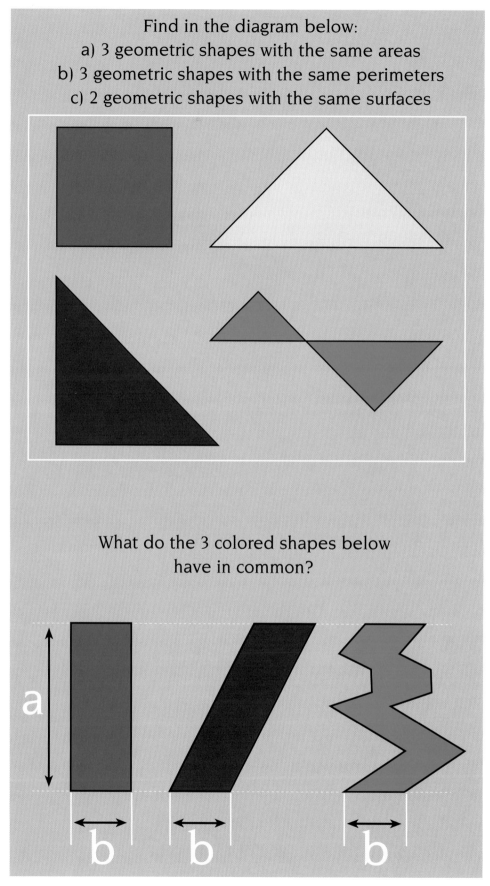

Shapes and identities

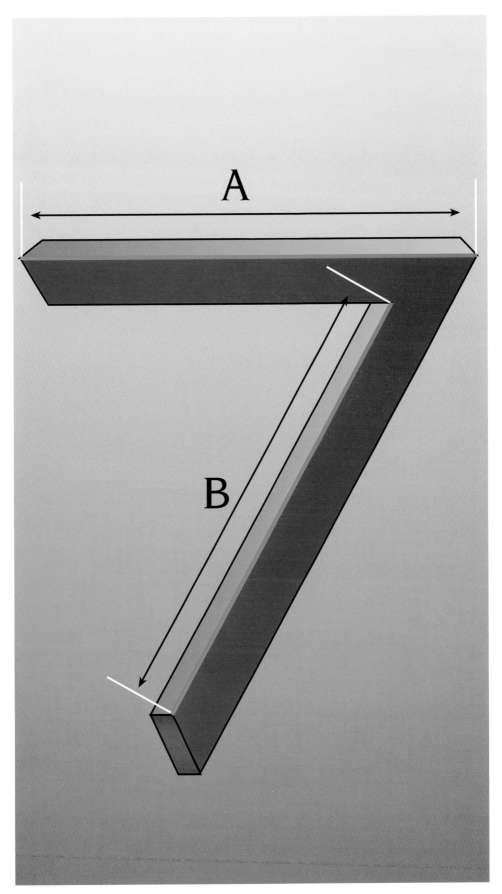

Is this figure possible?
Are green lines A and B the same length?

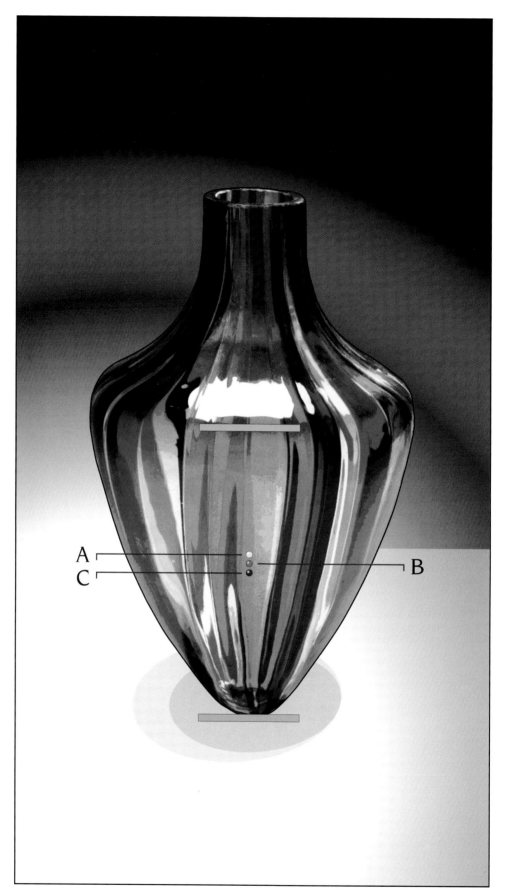

A

C

B

Which color dot is halfway up the distance between the 2 blue lines?

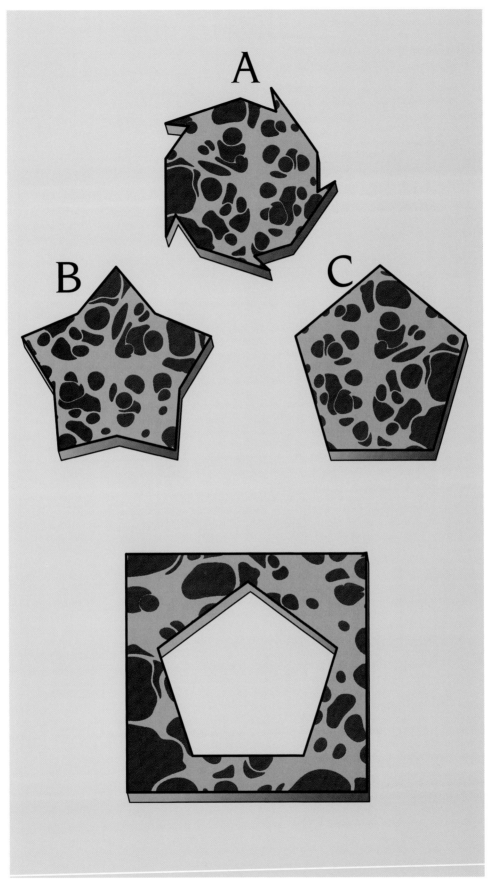

Which shape fits into the hole?

Solutions to Chapter 2

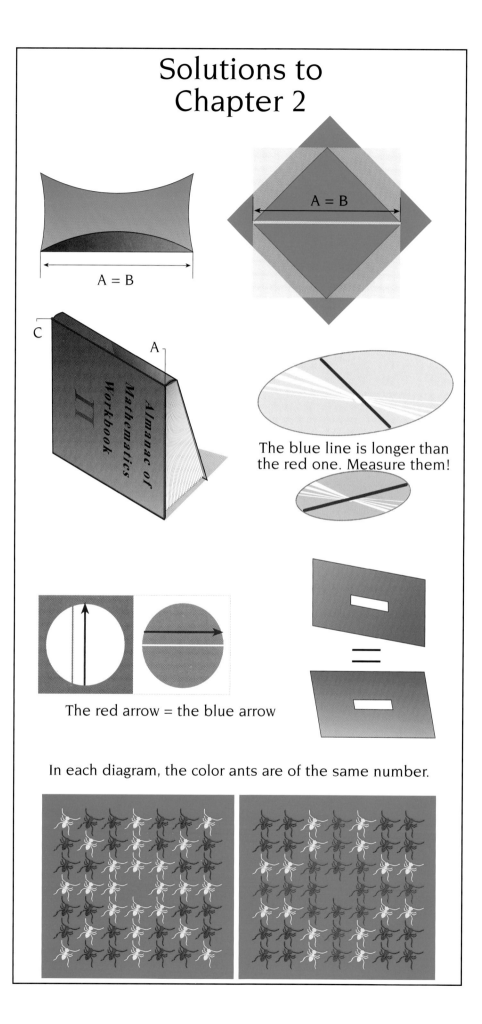

A = B

A = B

C

A

Almanac of Mathematics Workbook II

The blue line is longer than the red one. Measure them!

The red arrow = the blue arrow

=

In each diagram, the color ants are of the same number.

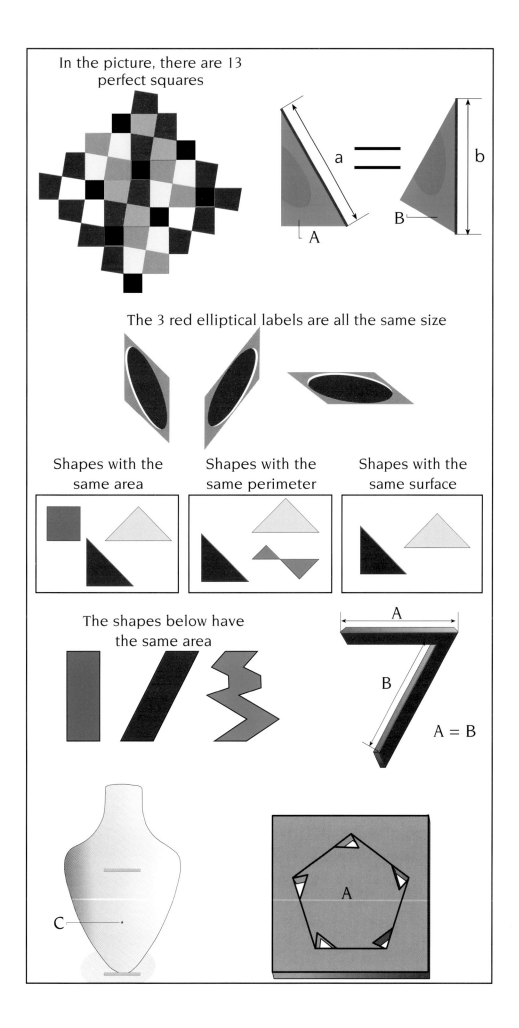

In the picture, there are 13 perfect squares

The 3 red elliptical labels are all the same size

Shapes with the same area

Shapes with the same perimeter

Shapes with the same surface

The shapes below have the same area

A = B

Chapter 3

Visual distortions

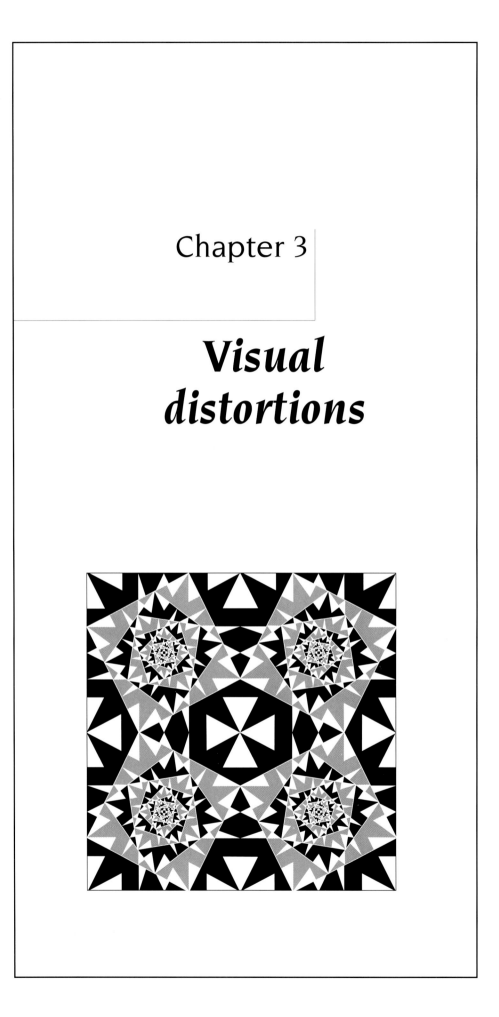

This kind of distortion is known as "geometric inversion."

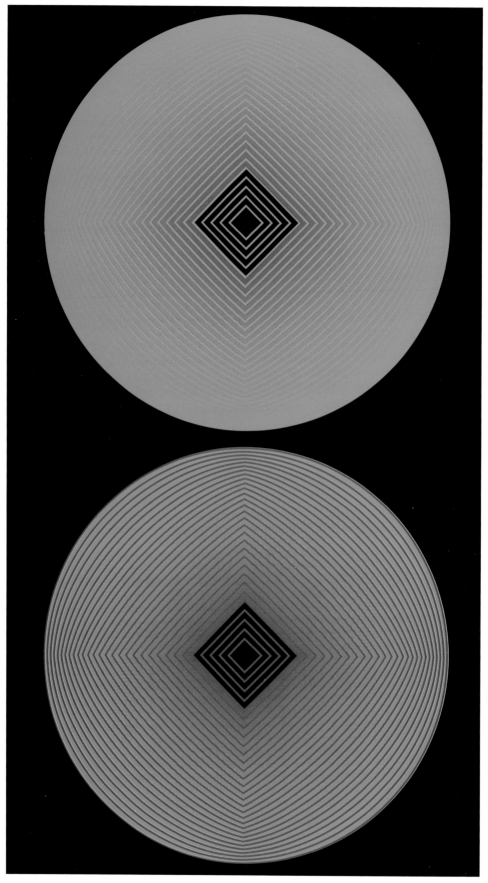

Squaring circles

Is anything here straight?

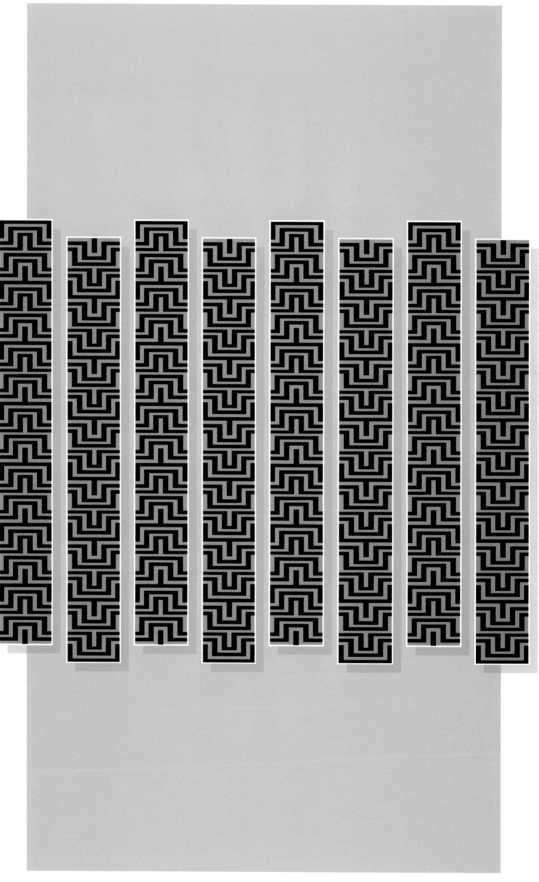

Are the slats perfectly parallel?

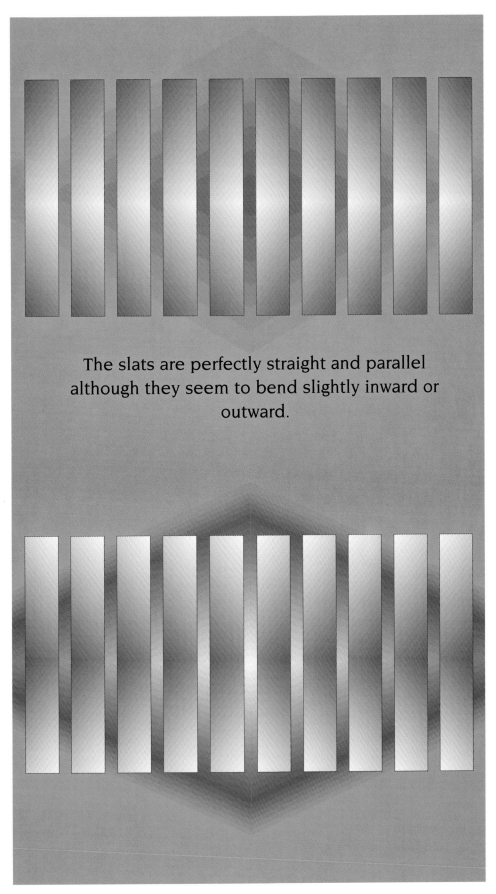

The slats are perfectly straight and parallel although they seem to bend slightly inward or outward.

Distortion experiments with shades

To see this image place silver paper rolled
into a cylinder in the white circle. Match the
cylinder's diameter to the circle's!

What is this?

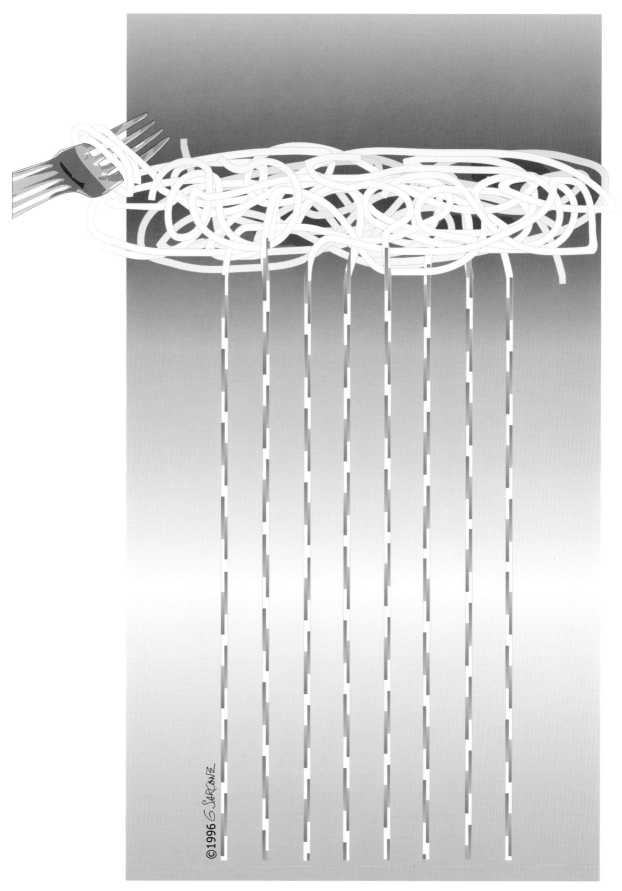

Do the vertical spaghettis bulge outward or inward?

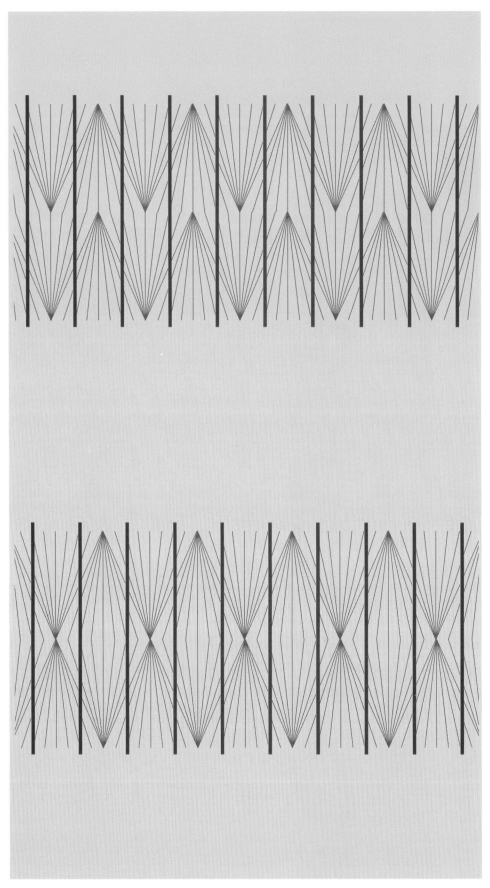

Are the red lines straight and parallel?

Are the rows of alternating color tiles above parallel?
Are the black lines in the figure below straight?

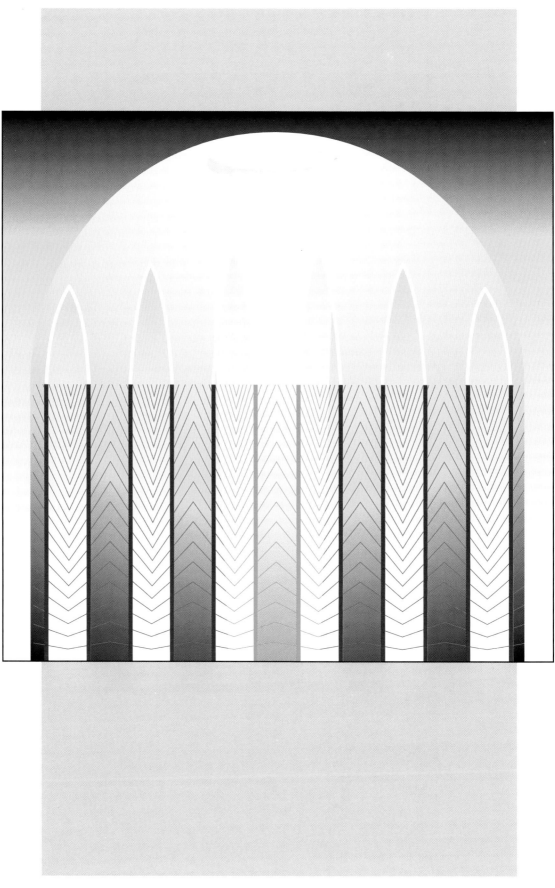

Do the red lines above tend to bend in at the top?
It's just an illusion.

Are the rows of alien rockets straight and parallel?

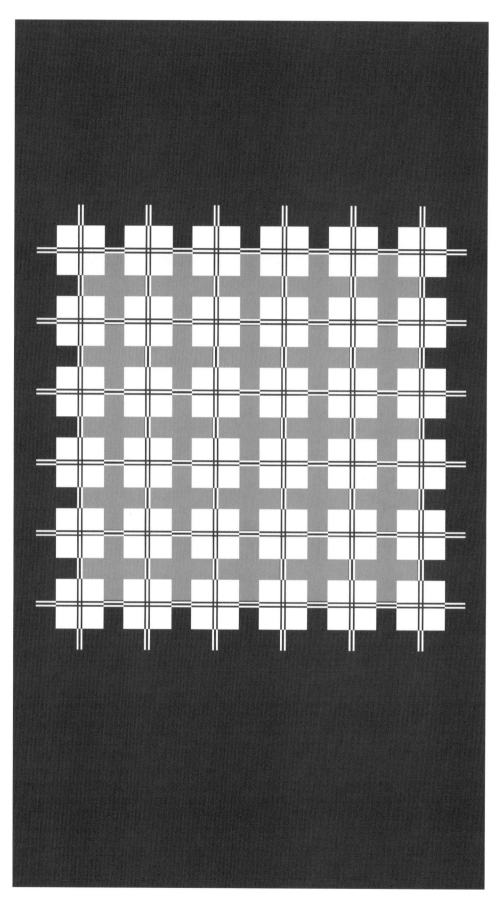

Are the lines of alternating color above straight?
Are the shapes between the lines really squares?

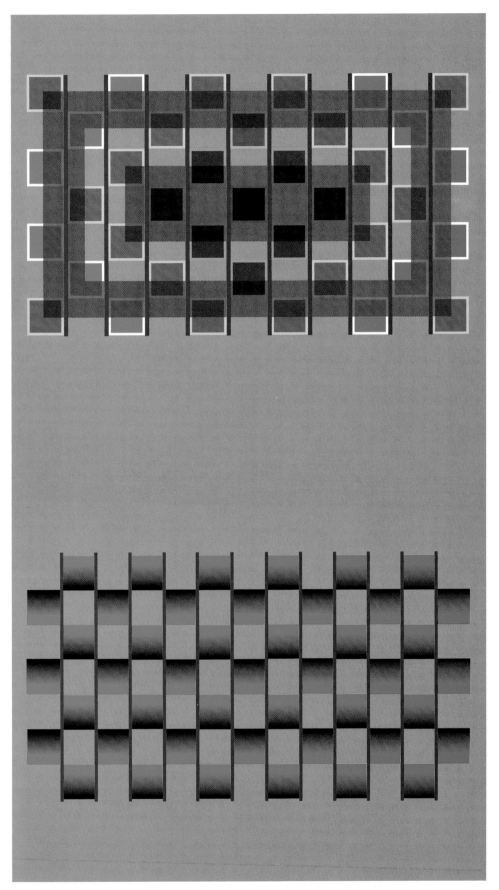

Are the vertical red lines straight and parallel to each other?

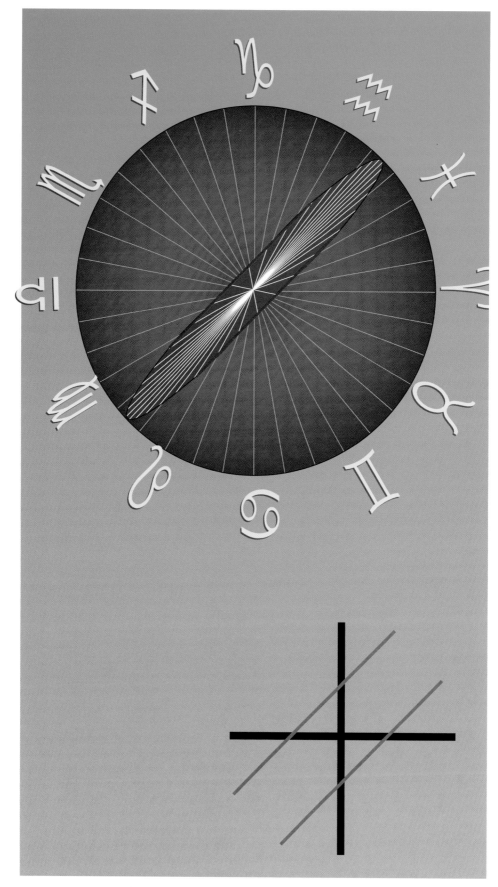

Are the parallel red lines really bowed?
The illusion works even with just two crossed lines!

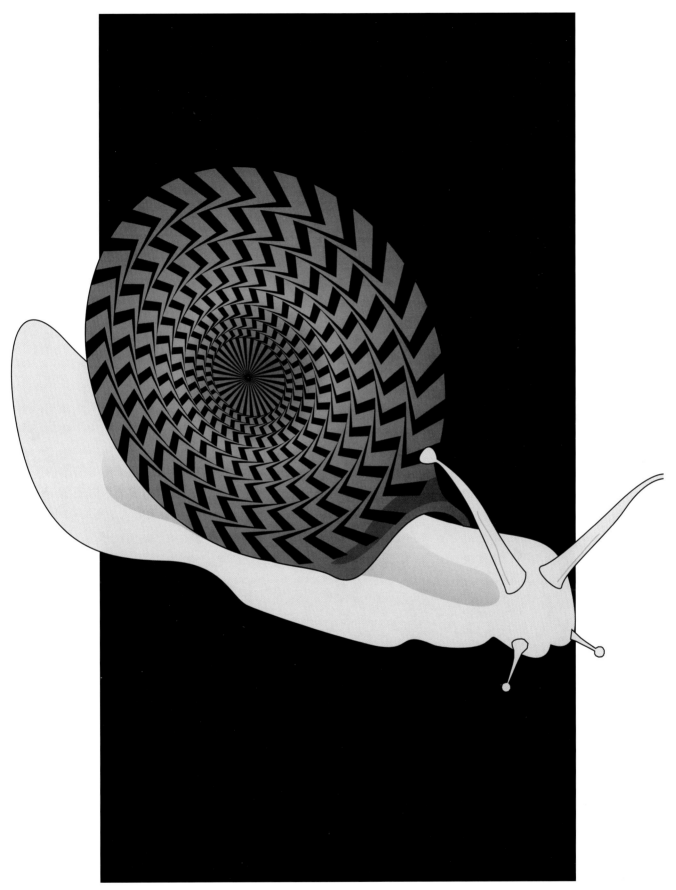

Is this snail shell really a spiral?

The parallel red lines seem to bulge inward, but they are perfectly straight.
A circle is enough to produce the illusion.

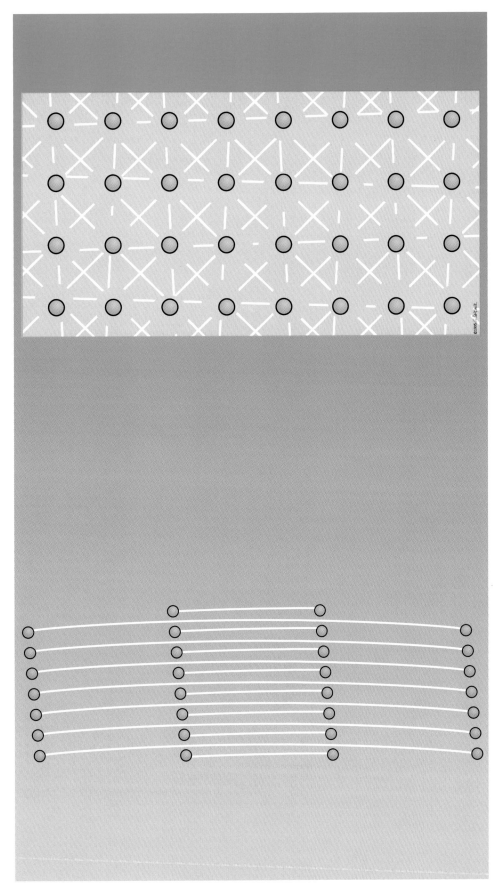

Undisciplined dots!
Are all the green dots of both diagrams aligned and parallel?

Solutions to Chapter 3

In this chapter all the lines, rows and slats are straight and parallel!

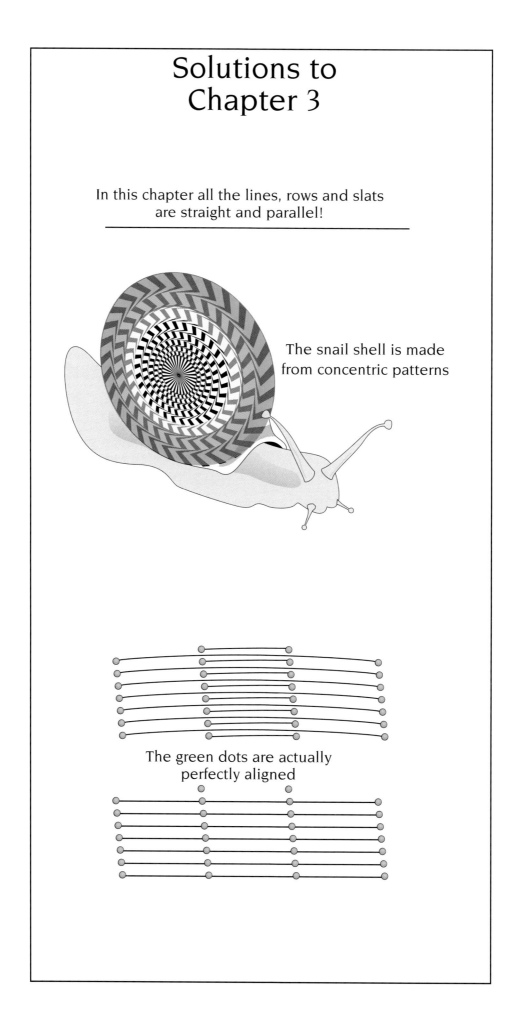

The snail shell is made from concentric patterns

The green dots are actually perfectly aligned

Chapter 4

Ambiguity, camouflages

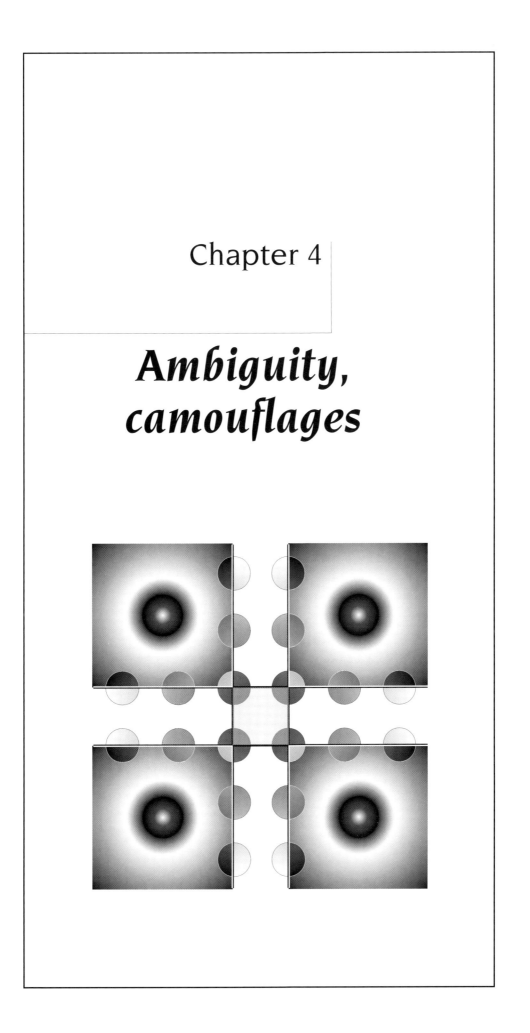

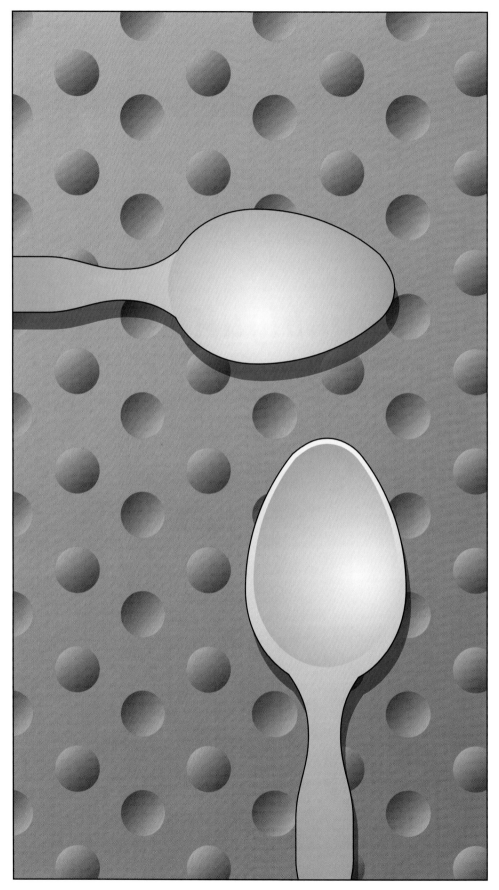

Convex or concave?

Polar bear crawling out of a water hole in the ice or sea lion?

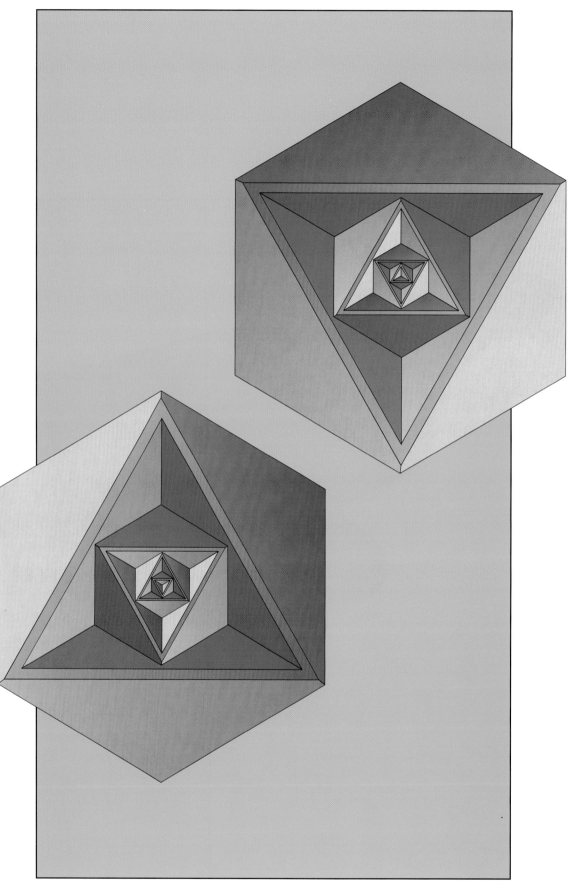

Japanese boxes

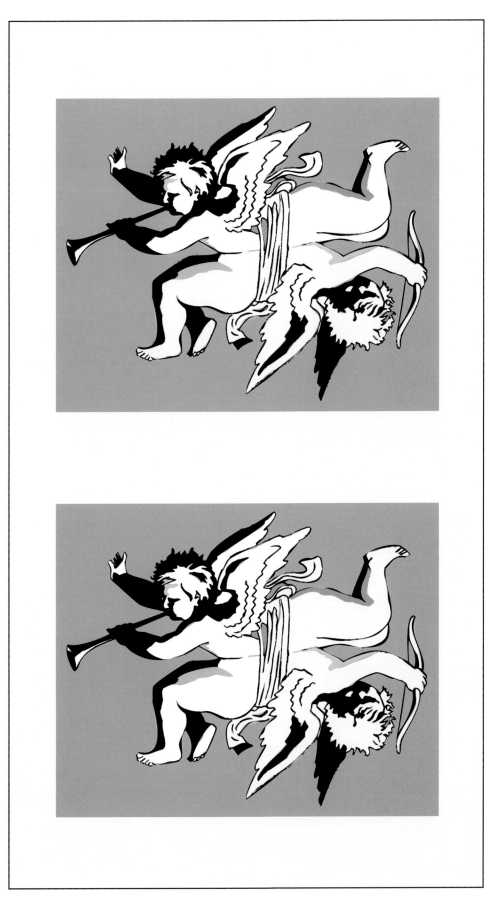

How many angels?

Do you see circles or spirals?

Find the donkey in the monkeys.

Reverse City

Is the background of this circuit board red or blue?

Pink flamingo, or Indian elephant?
Turn the page upside down.

Concentric ellipses or spirals?

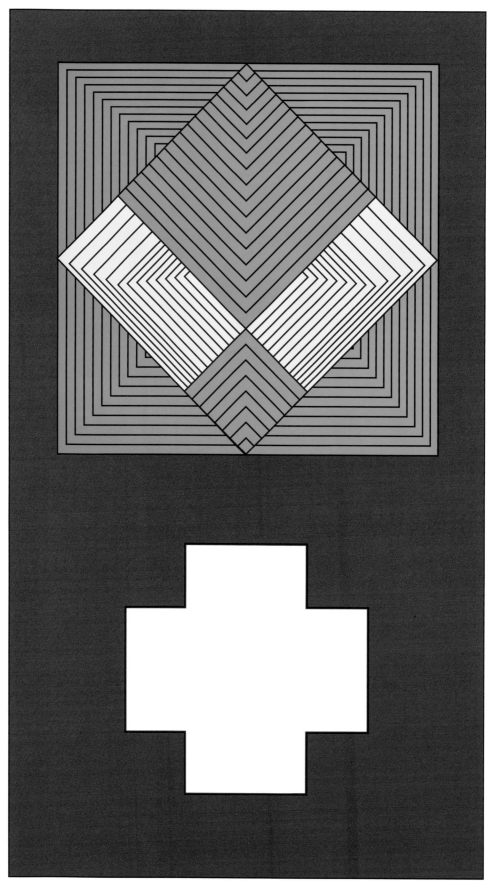

Find the cross in the square.

Do you see floating squares, or is it just your imagination?

How many birds can you find above?
Do you see a road or a river? Maybe both?

How many faces?

Do you see one face, or two, or three above?
How many glasses do you see?

abcdefg

hijklmn

opqrstu

vwxyz

Martian alphabet? No, just a minimal perceptible font.

Stripes reveal a zebra.

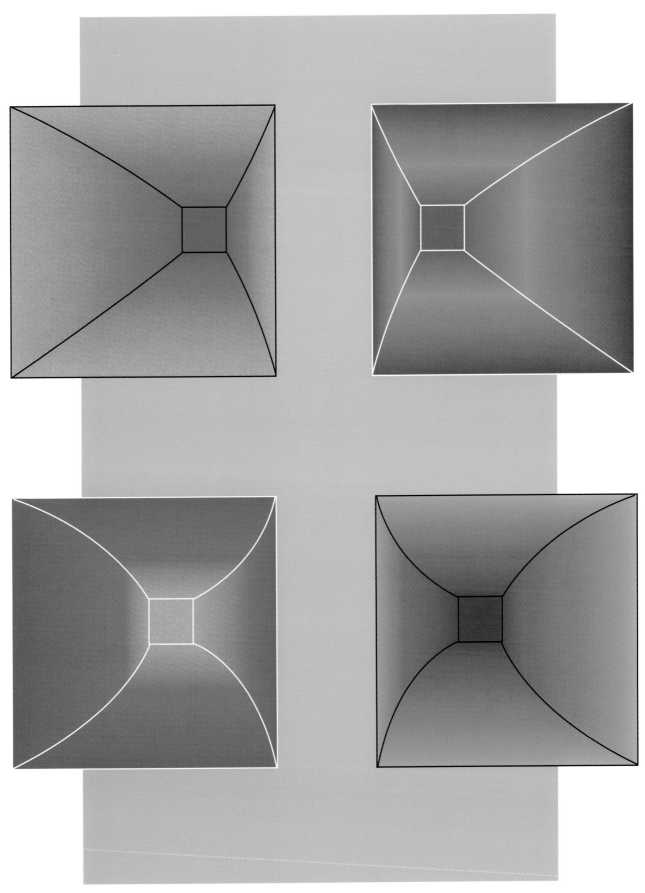

Coming out or going in?

Are you looking at this woman from behind or face on?
Hide the shaded arm with a pencil to enhance the effect.

Spiralling cubes

A network of rectangles can make circles.

Three temples make an apparent cube.

A few shadows in empty space define a cube.

What can you see? 1) A square in a 3-D space?
2) Two pyramids with a square base? 3) Two pyramids with a triangular base?

None of the squares in this picture is really there!
Reality isn't always WYSIWYG.

98

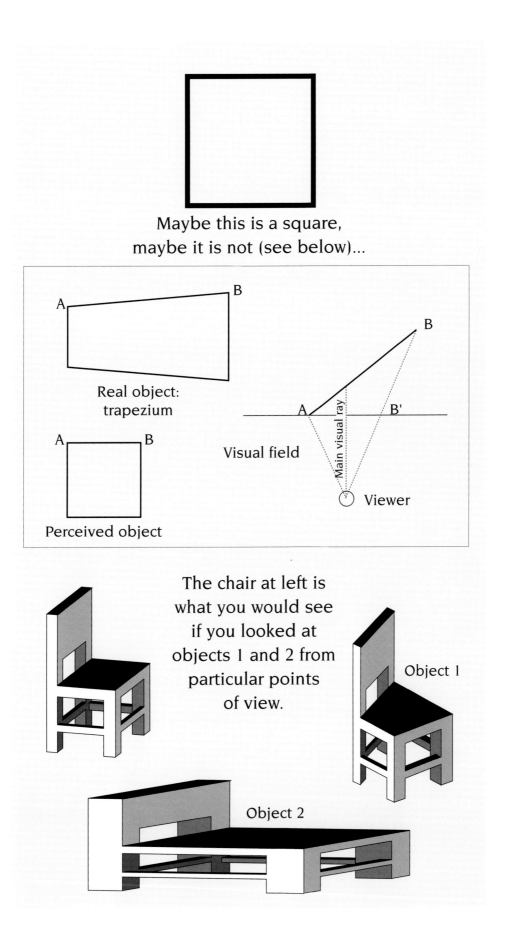

Maybe this is a square,
maybe it is not (see below)...

A   B

Real object:
trapezium

A   B

Perceived object

B

A   B'

Main visual ray

Visual field

Viewer

The chair at left is
what you would see
if you looked at
objects 1 and 2 from
particular points
of view.

Object 1

Object 2

How many ships do you see above?
Actually, there is just one with optical camouflage (see below).

These Mona Lisas seem to be looking in different directions, even though the eyes of both are identical and have exactly the same orientation!

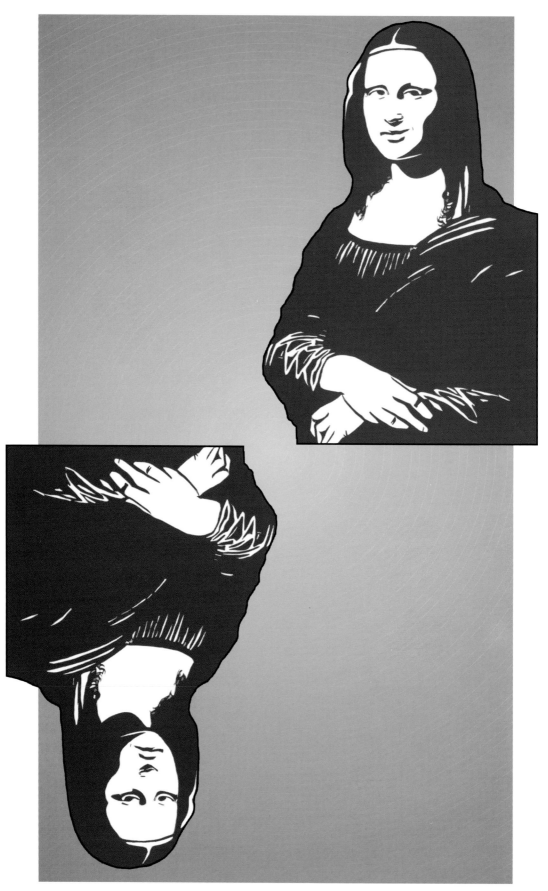

Is something wrong with the bottom image? If you turn
the book upside down, you'll see the eyes and mouth are inverted.

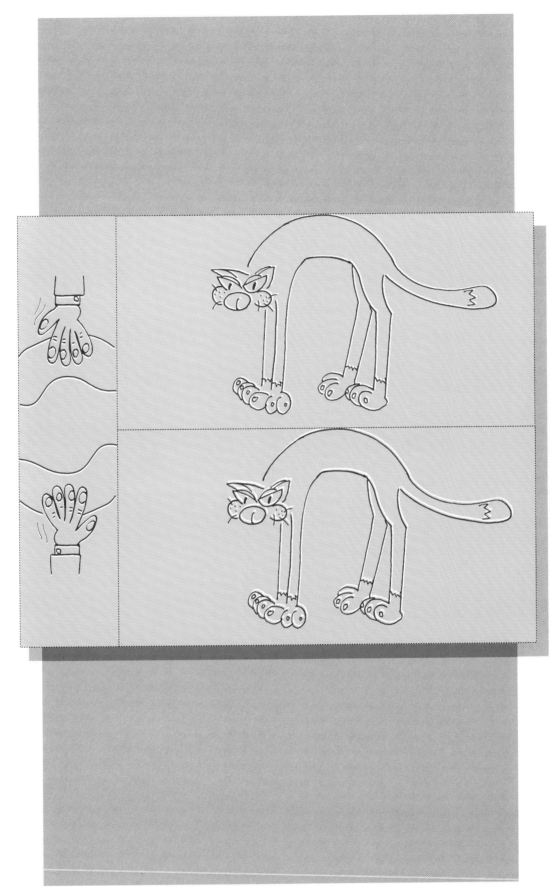

Can you cut the picture into 3 pieces along the dotted lines and rearrange them
to make the hands stroke both purring cats?

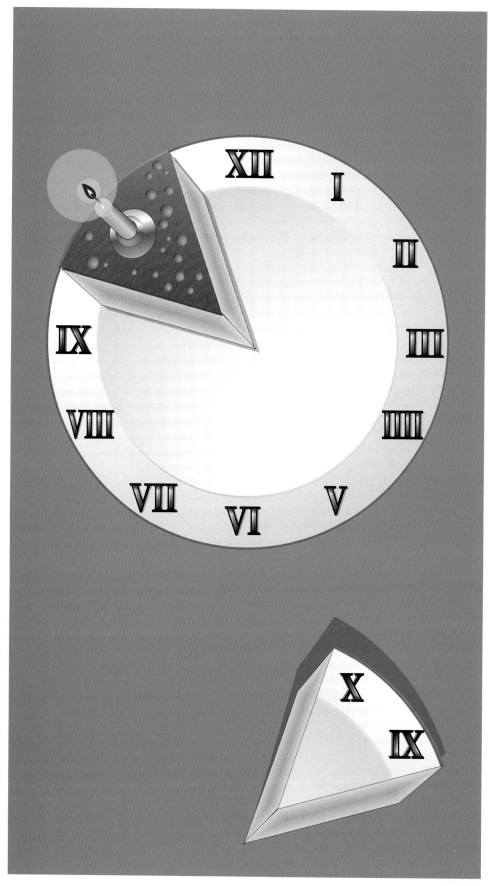

A slice of cake or a slice out of time?
This birthday cake seems to make time go backward.

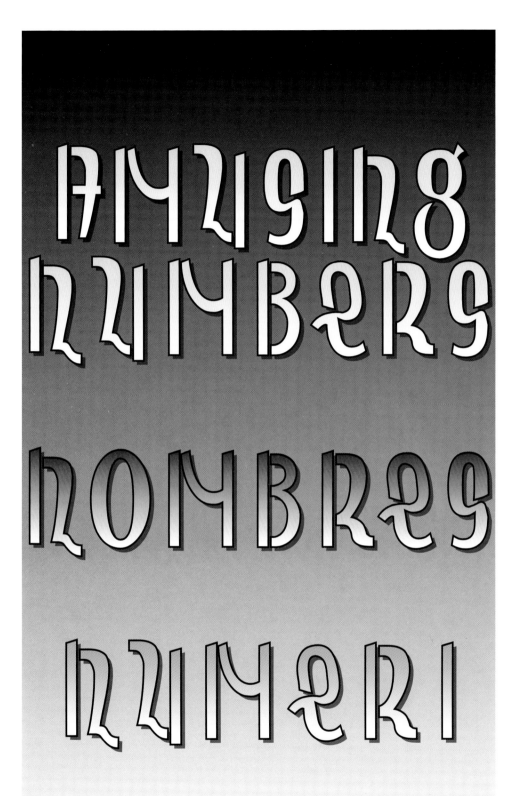

Letters or numbers?
(in English, French, and Italian)

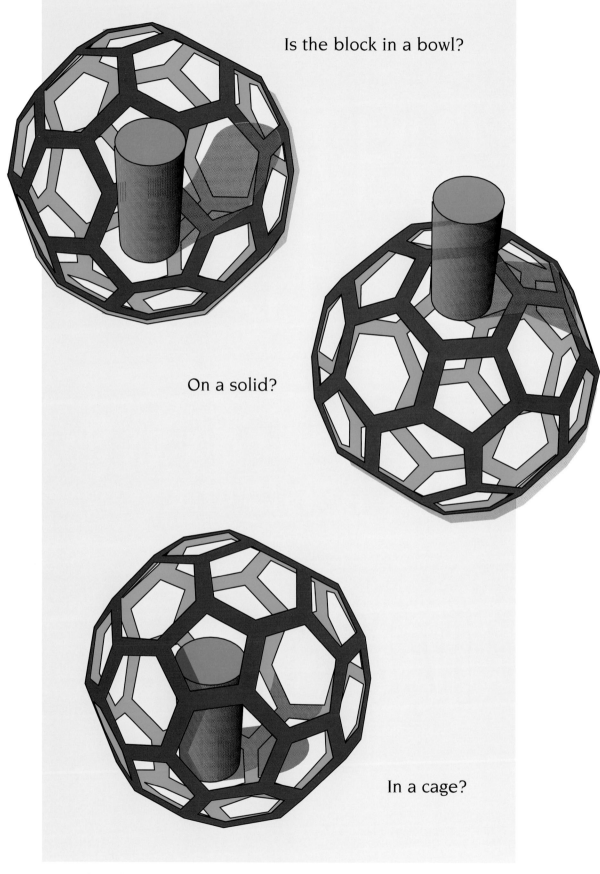

Is the block in a bowl?

On a solid?

In a cage?

The shadow of the cylinder makes the other figure
look like three different shapes.

Find 3 faces.

Find the violins in the rungs
of the parapet.

Hidden figures

Bald egg and long-haired egg? Are they of the same size?
Actually, this is a woman's head seen from above.

The red figure partially concealed
by the black squares could be one
of three regular geometric shapes.
What are they?

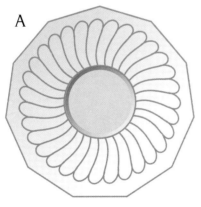

A

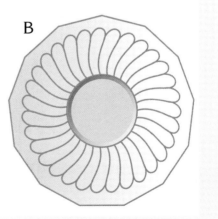

B

Find 3 differences
between pictures
A and B.

Test your shape recognition aptitude.

What is the fundamental difference between the decorative spirals in *katoptrons* (antique Greek mirrors) A and B?

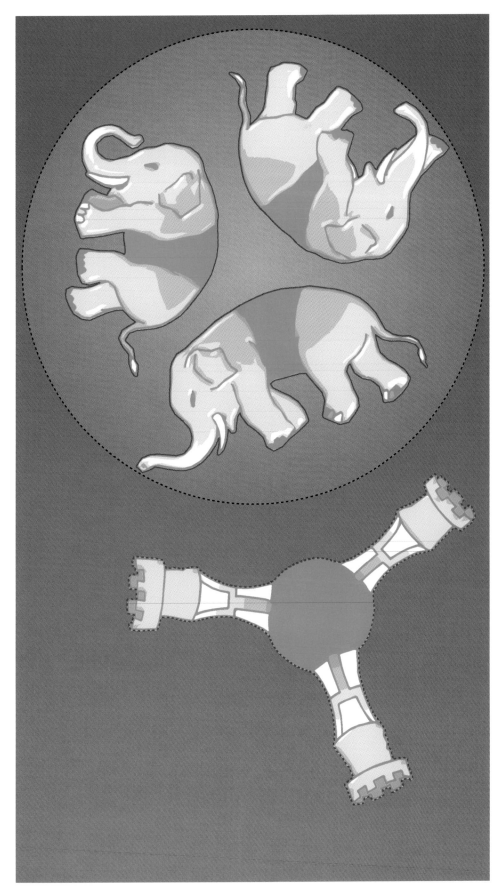

Photocopy and cut out the puzzle elements along the dotted lines. Then arrange the pieces to fit the 3 towers on the backs of the elephants.

111

Op art illusion
Find 4 discs in the picture above.

Solutions to Chapter 4

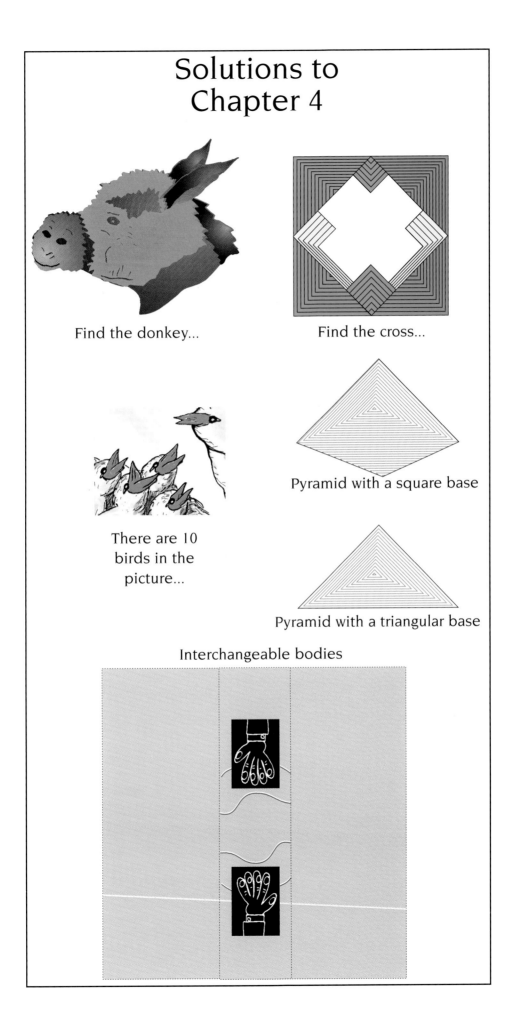

Find the donkey...

Find the cross...

Pyramid with a square base

There are 10 birds in the picture...

Pyramid with a triangular base

Interchangeable bodies

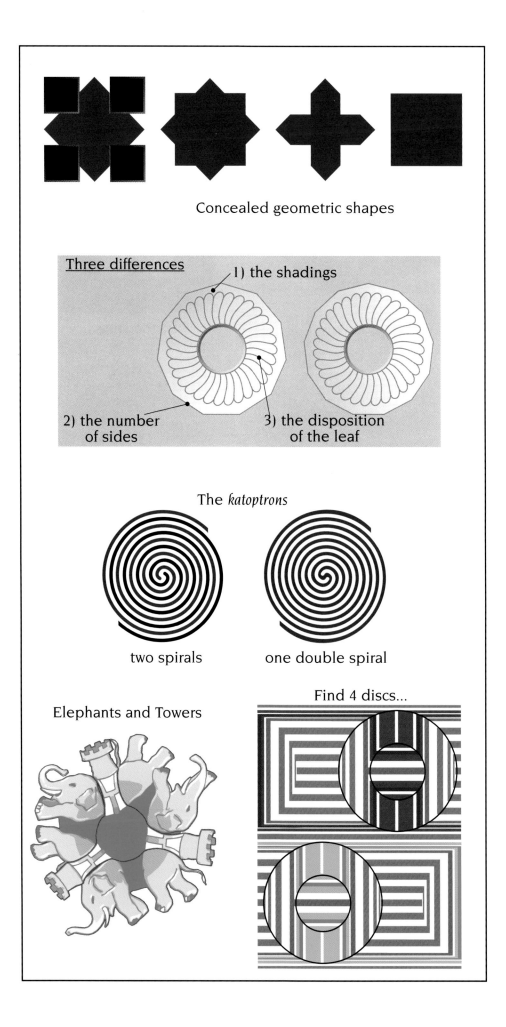

Concealed geometric shapes

Three differences

1) the shadings

2) the number of sides

3) the disposition of the leaf

The *katoptrons*

two spirals

one double spiral

Elephants and Towers

Find 4 discs...

Chapter 5

Impossible figures, paradoxes

Cubamid or pyrube?

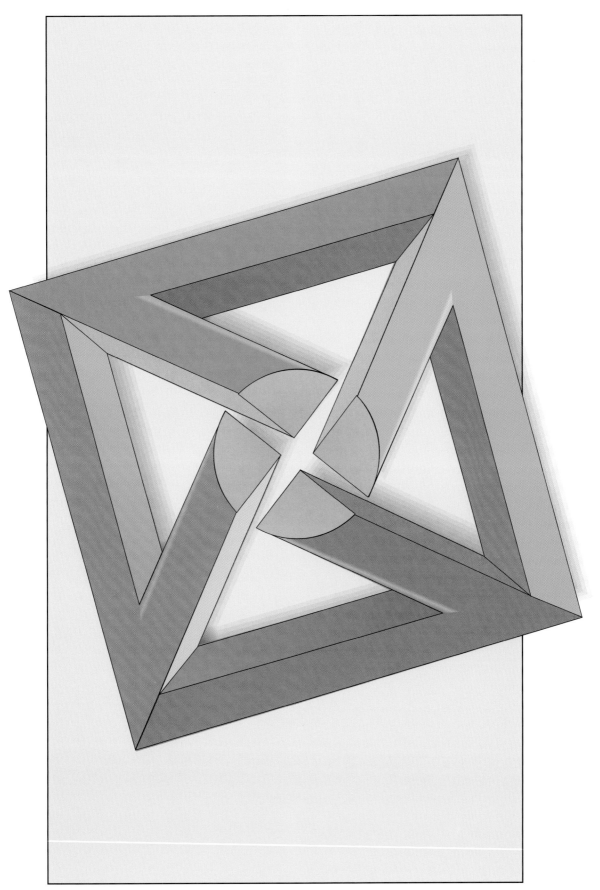

An impossible solid?

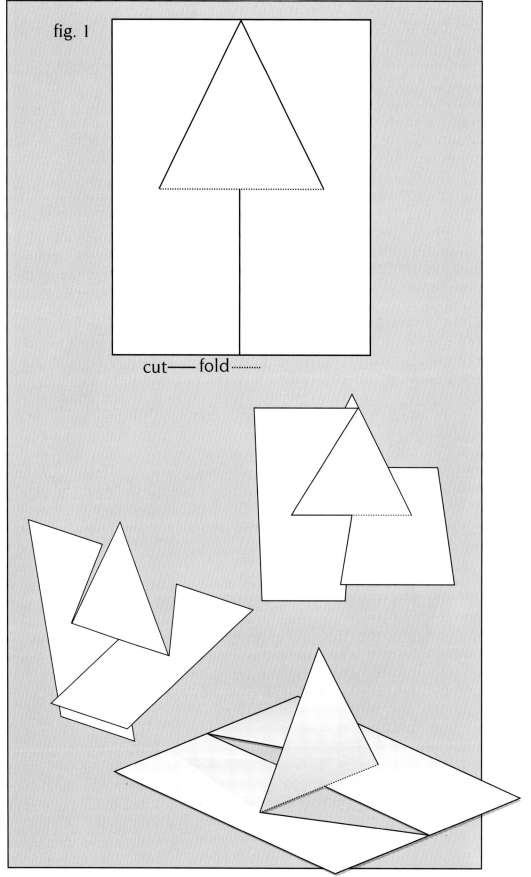

fig. 1

cut——fold··········

Copy the diagram in fig. 1. Then cut it along the 3 lines indicated and fold it as shown above into an impossible pyramid.

Copy and cut out the 4 geometric shapes above.
Then assemble them to form a cross. Impossible?

Impossible structures

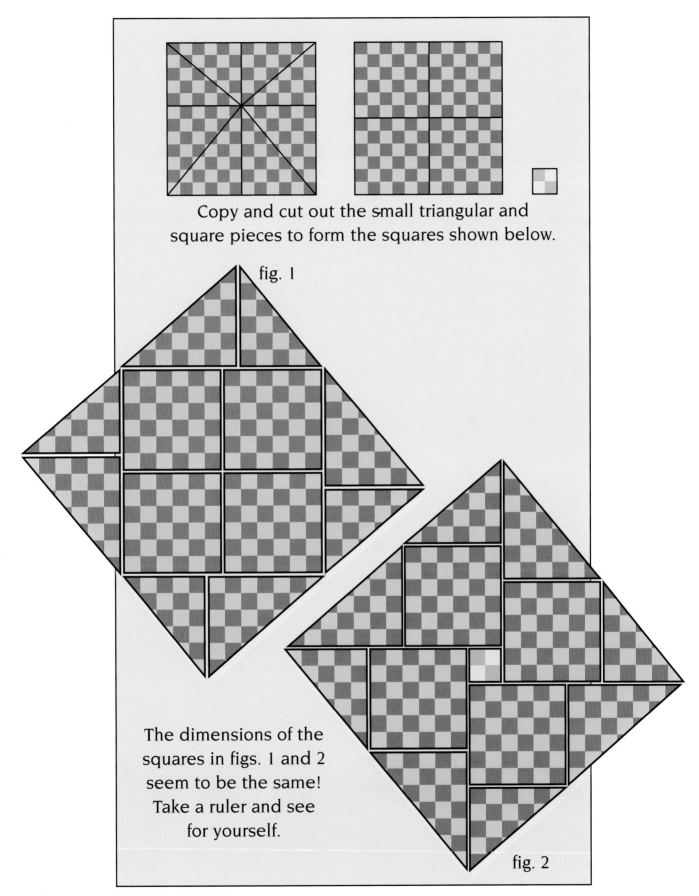

Copy and cut out the small triangular and square pieces to form the squares shown below.

fig. 1

fig. 2

The dimensions of the squares in figs. 1 and 2 seem to be the same! Take a ruler and see for yourself.

Both squares are formed with the same pieces.
The second one, however, needs an extra piece! Why?

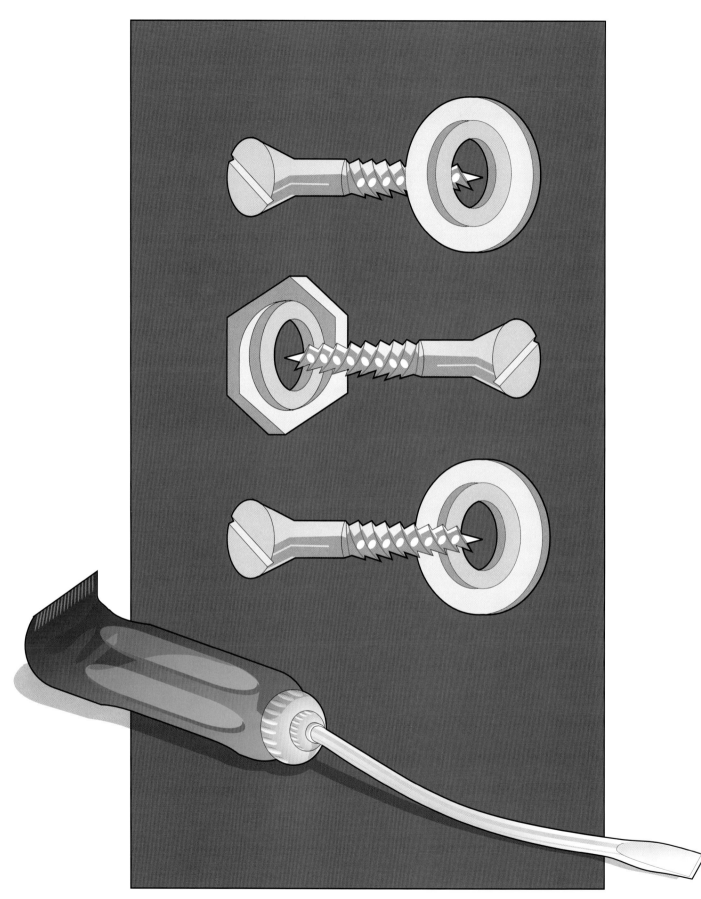

Improbable screws and washers...
plus a tube of screwdriver-paste

Do you perceive an impossible hexagonal structure?

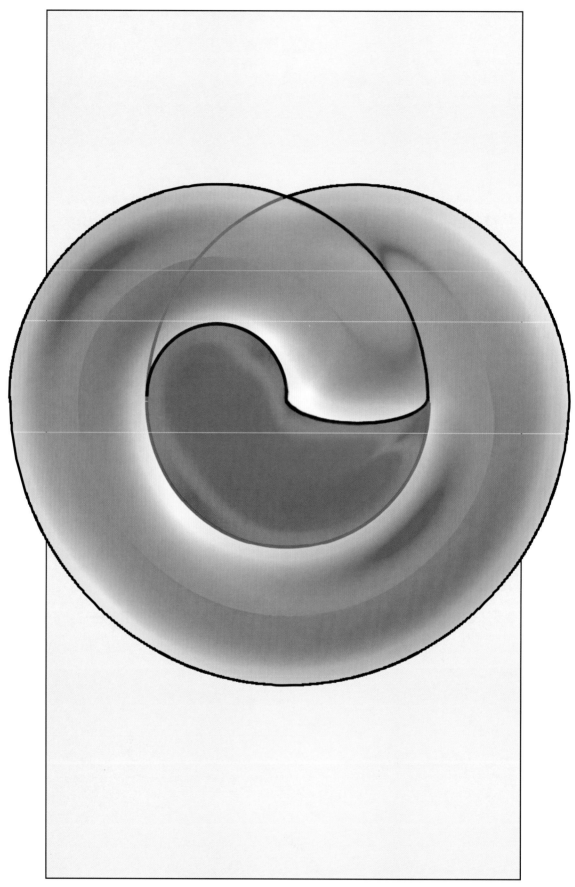

Impossible object: a tubular phial

The vanishing birds: Cut out pieces A, B and C of this illusion puzzle.
Then lay them out so that one more bird appears!

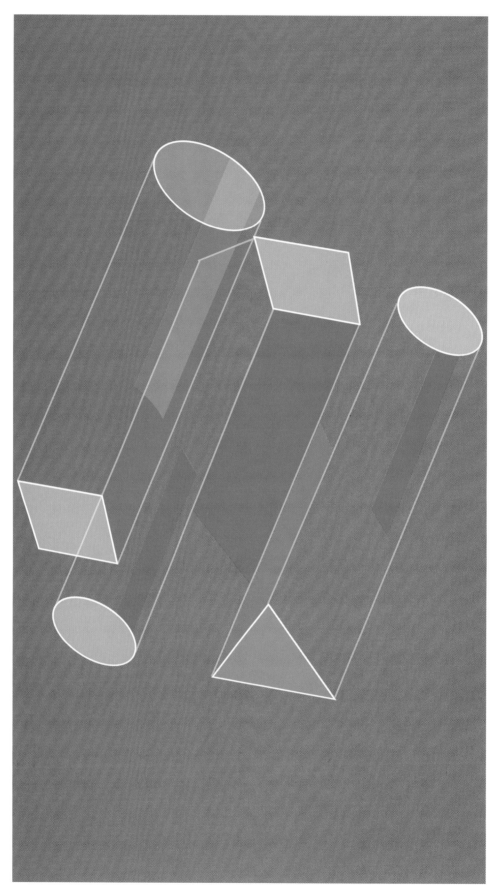

Impossible prisms and cylinders

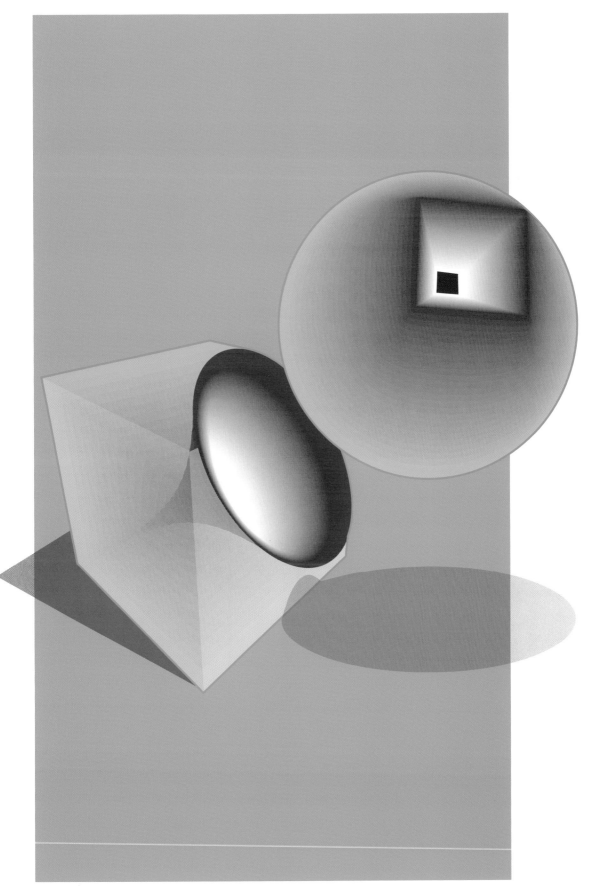

Improbable squarings

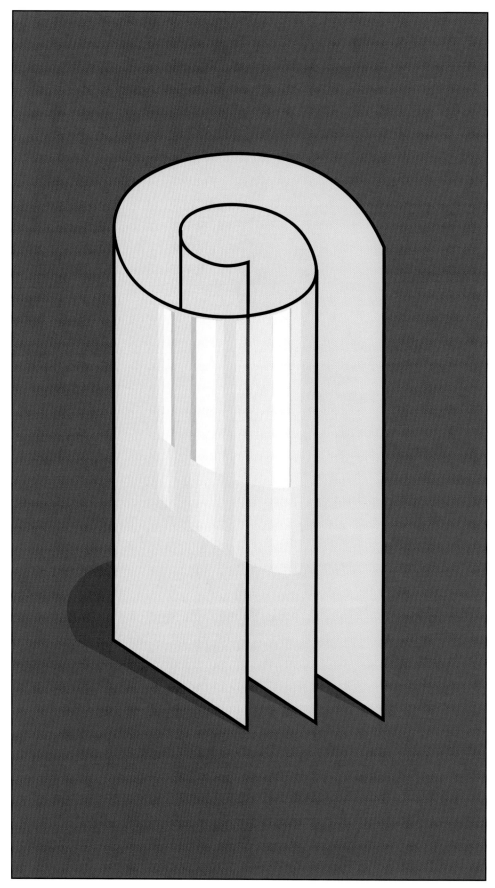

A right-angled spiral

Impossible Chinese dice on an unreal Chinese table

129

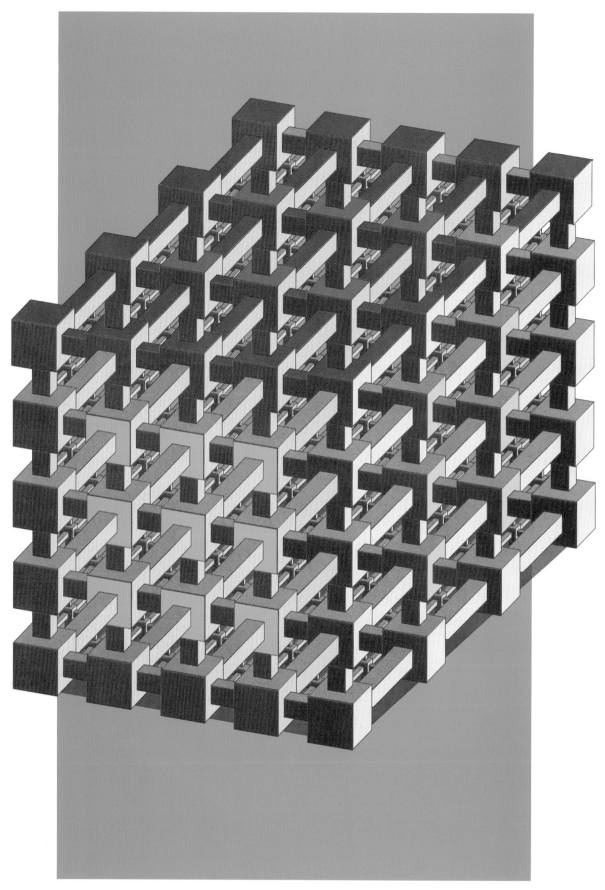

Peculiar cubic network

The tangramagic puzzle is made from 10 pieces (a 7-piece tangram + 2 L-shaped pieces + 1 small square). Cut out these 10 pieces and put them together in order to make the Japanese writing "sekishu no koe" appear. Do you notice anything funny?

Cut out the 10 pieces along the dotted lines

Assemble the rectangle making the Japanese writing above appear

The incredible tangramagic puzzle

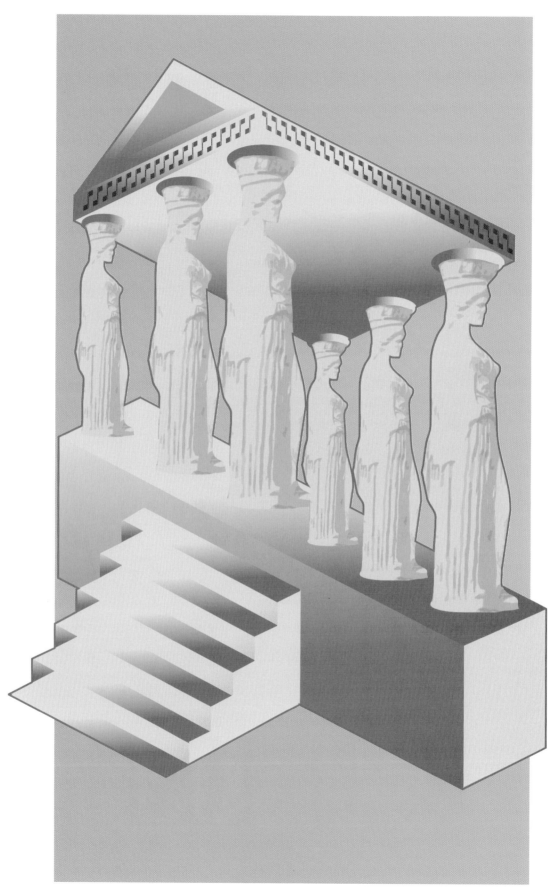

A linear temple

An illusive labyrinth! a) Find a path to free the green dot.
b) Draw a line that joins the small blue squares.

Find 4 optical oddities!

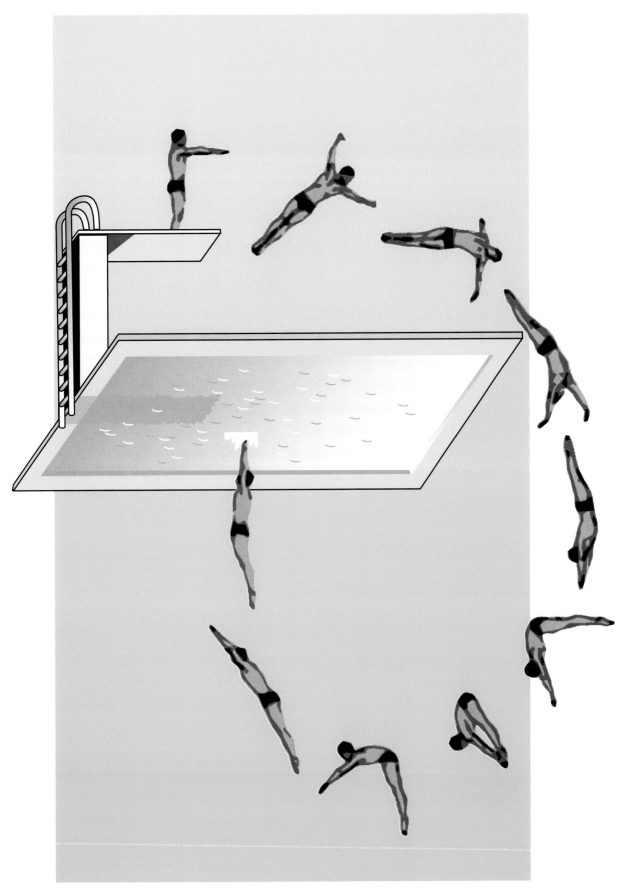

Bilateral swimming pool
Turn the book upside-down.

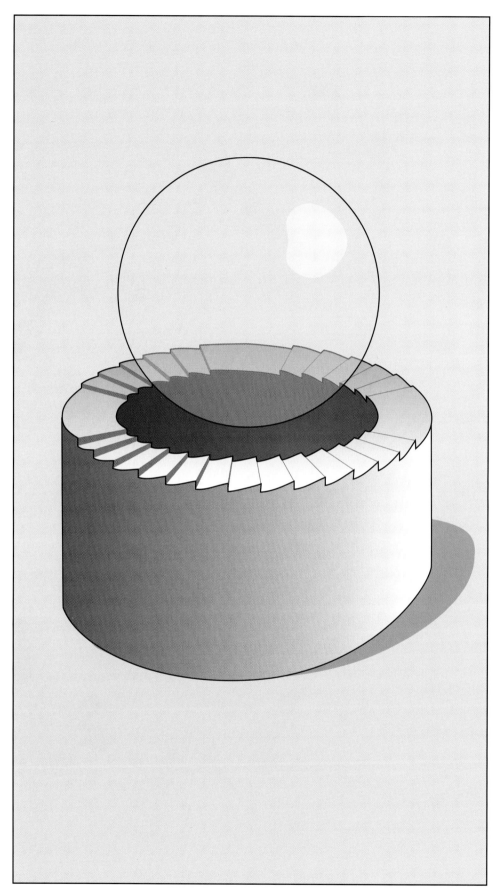

Observe this magic circular staircase. If you go downstairs, what happens?

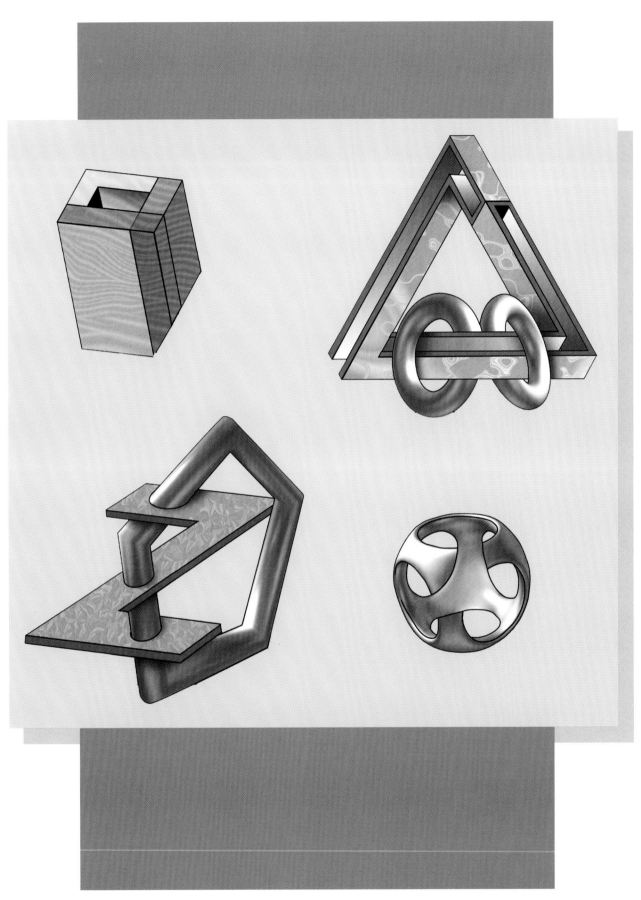

Four impossible objects. Or, is the top left just perspective?

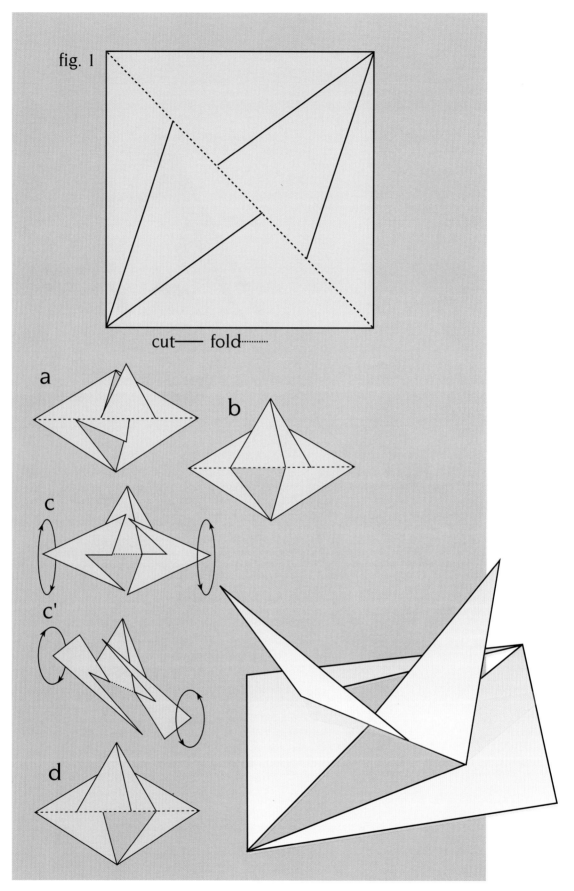

fig. 1

cut —— fold ········

a

b

c

c'

d

Copy the diagram in fig. 1. Then cut along the 4 lines indicated
and fold it as shown into an impossible figure.

To make an incredible magic card,
follow the instructions below.

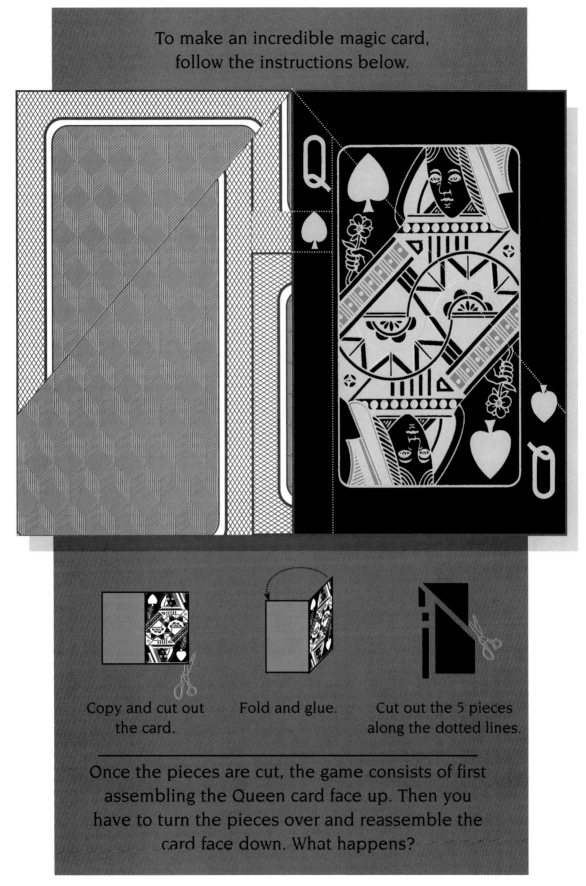

Copy and cut out
the card.

Fold and glue.

Cut out the 5 pieces
along the dotted lines.

Once the pieces are cut, the game consists of first
assembling the Queen card face up. Then you
have to turn the pieces over and reassemble the
card face down. What happens?

The Queen of Illusion

Solutions to Chapter 5

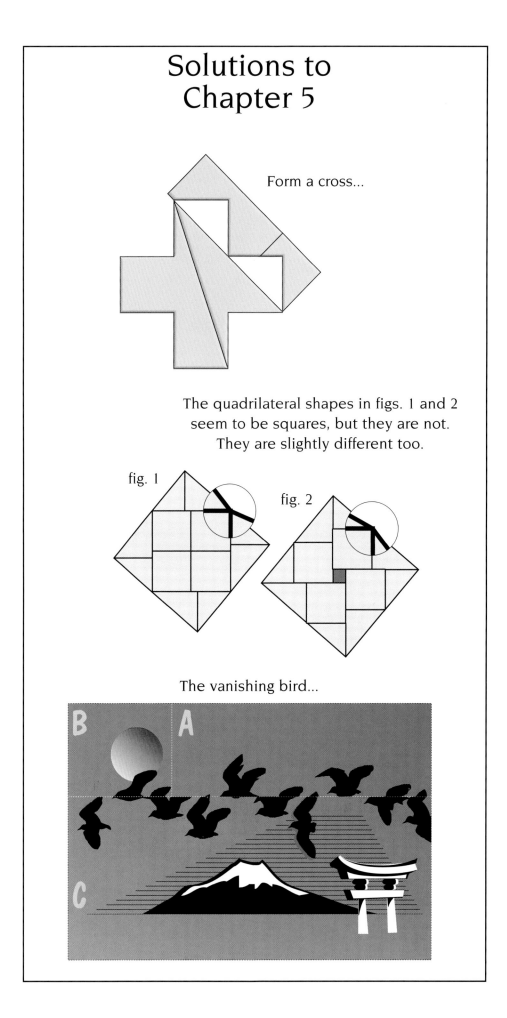

Form a cross...

The quadrilateral shapes in figs. 1 and 2
seem to be squares, but they are not.
They are slightly different too.

fig. 1

fig. 2

The vanishing bird...

B   A

C

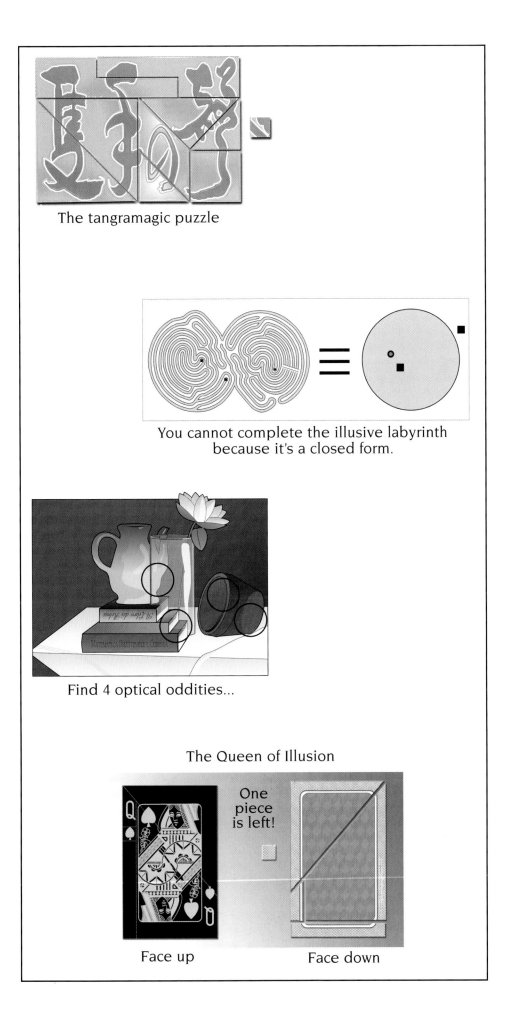

The tangramagic puzzle

You cannot complete the illusive labyrinth because it's a closed form.

Find 4 optical oddities...

The Queen of Illusion

One piece is left!

Face up

Face down

Chapter 6

Kinetic illusions, moving patterns

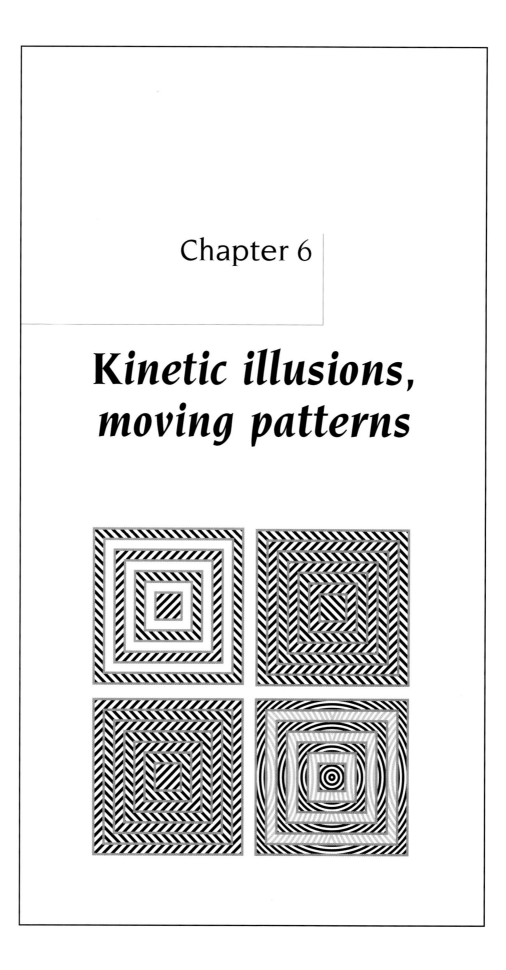

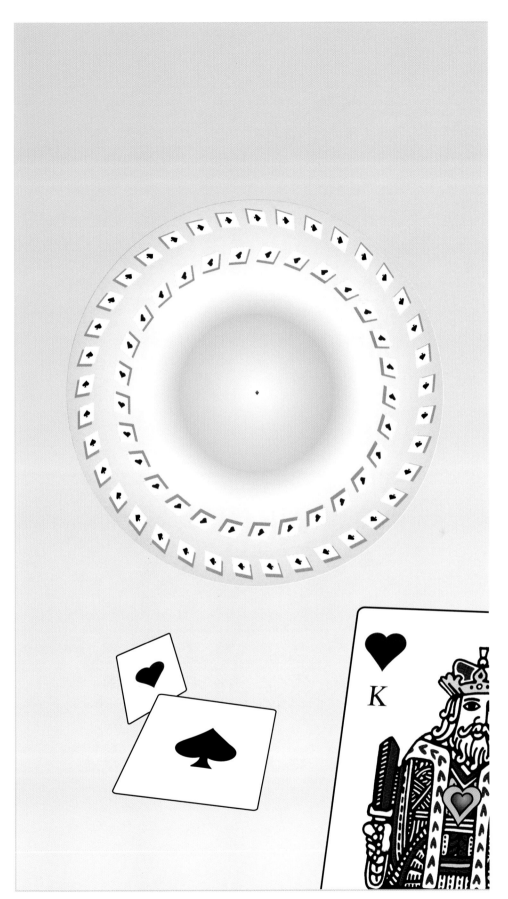

Stare at the tiny spade in the middle of the disc and slowly bring it toward your eyes. What happens?

Concentrate on the central cross of one of the discs, while shaking the image slightly and you'll see the cross floating.

- Print out the model above and paste it onto a piece of cardboard, then cut out the disc.
- Push a short, pointed pencil through its center.
- Hold the top of the pencil lightly, spin the disc and then let go.
- You'll notice that the rotating disc gives intermittent stimulation to color receptors in the eye, producing a <u>subjective illusion of color</u>.

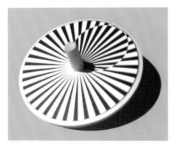 

Subjective color illusion I

Subjective color illusion II
Follow the instructions on the previous page.

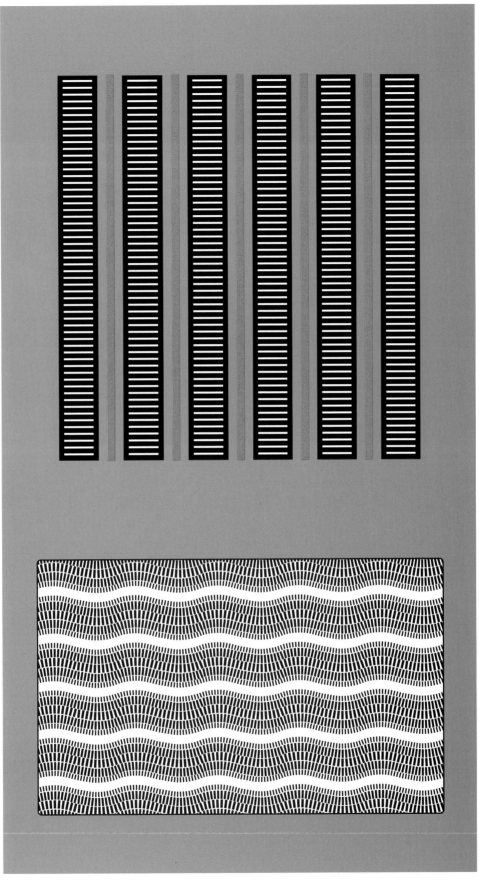

Do the red lines twist up and down?
Do the curved white lines seem to vibrate and blink forward and backward?

If you concentrate on the circular colored bands,
you may see a vibrating fluid.

- Copy the model above and paste it onto cardboard, then cut out the disc.
- Push a short, pointed pencil through its center.
- Hold the top of the pencil lightly, spin the disc and then let go.
- You'll notice that the spirals in the disc seem to pulsate!

The conflicting spirals

Observe the image while rotating the page. You may see some color tints!

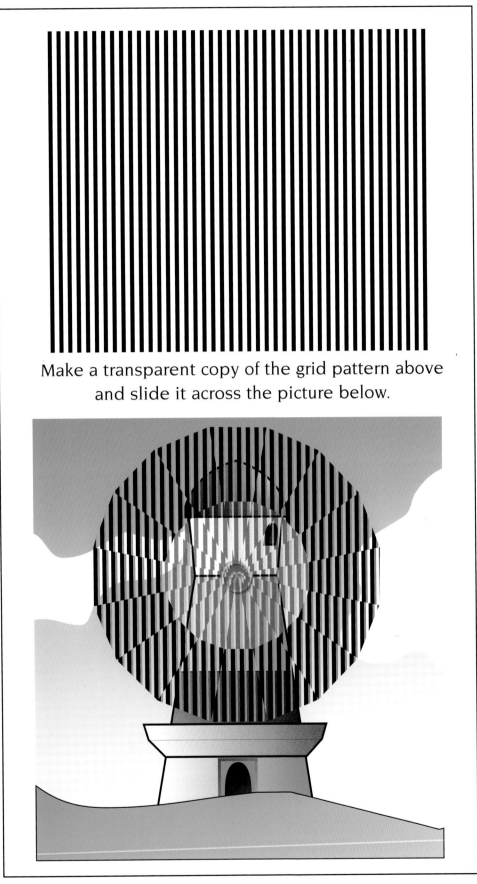

Make a transparent copy of the grid pattern above
and slide it across the picture below.

Transform linear movement into circular movement.
Make the blades of the windmill rotate.

Make a top with the pattern below. Put on 3-D glasses (with blue and red lenses) and spin the top slowly. Close your left and right eyes alternately while you watch the top rotating. What happens?

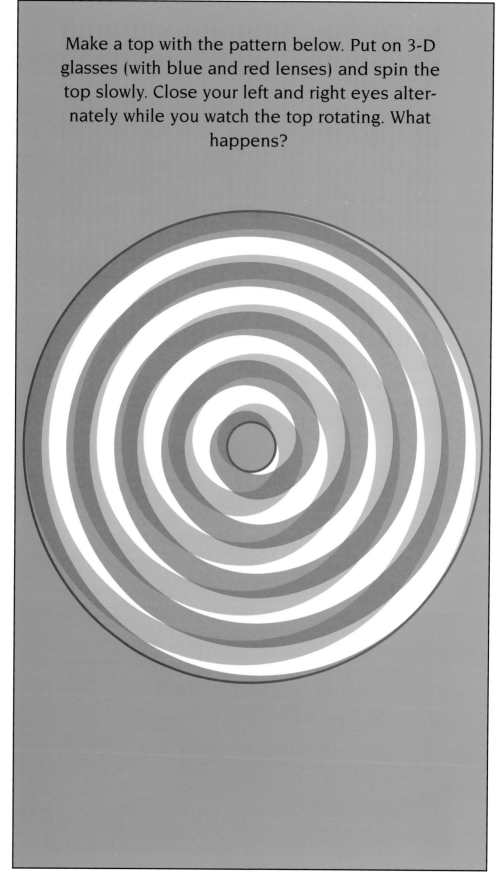

3-D top

Chapter 7

A *potpourri*
of illusions

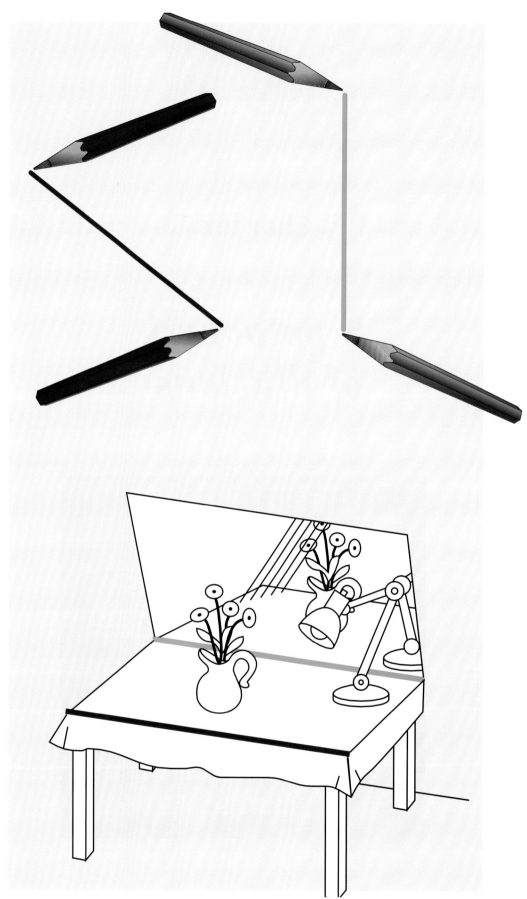

It is hard to believe, but the red and blue lines are the same length.

Every way is up in this impossible drawing.

The door is opening in and out at the same time.
And that is just the first mystery here.

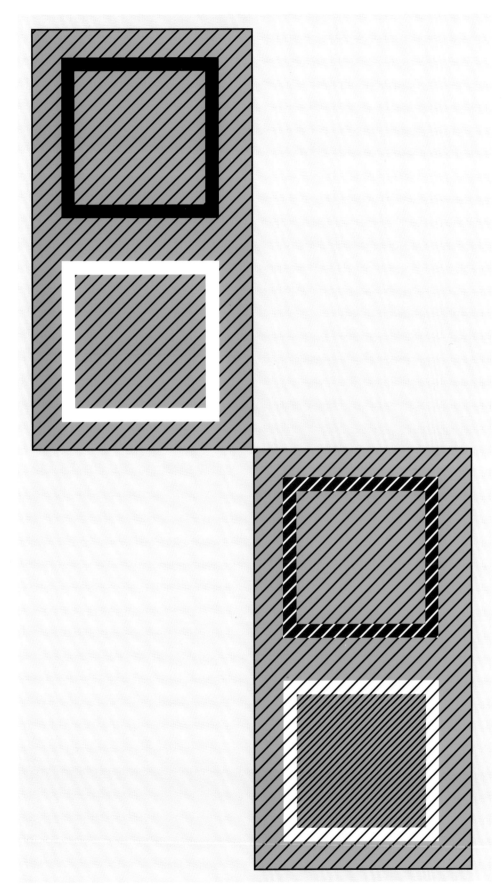

In the squares at the top the diagonals seem to run straight behind both squares. But see what happens below when the diagonals are connected.

Move the picture from side to side.

Follow the directions to make the top spin.

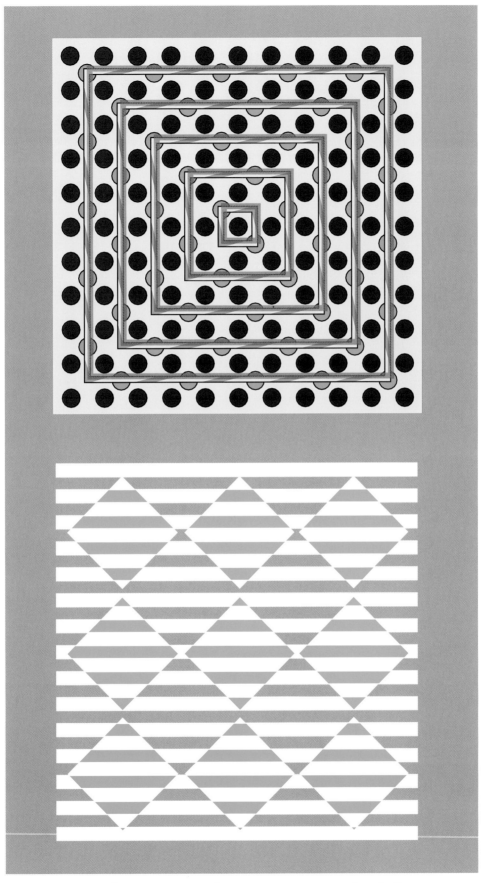

Are the squares above twisting to the left?
Are the lines below straight or wavy.

Index